North American Furbearers
A Contemporary Reference

North American Furbearers
A Contemporary Reference

Edited by

Eugene F. Deems, Jr. and Duane Pursley

1983

Published by the International Association of Fish and Wildlife Agencies
in cooperation with
the Maryland Department of Natural Resources-Wildlife Administration

ACKNOWLEDGEMENTS

The production of this book began in 1978 and involved over eighty professional wildlife specialists throughout the United States and Canada.

Sincere appreciation is extended to the authors of the following species sections:

Opossum
Ronald D. Andrews — Iowa Conservation Commission, Iowa

Beaver
Kent E. Klepinger and Ned Norton — Department of Natural Resources, Wisconsin
David J. Cartwright — Department of Natural Resources, New Brunswick

Muskrat
Chet McCord — Division of Fish and Wildlife, Massachusetts
Richard R. P. Stardom — Department of Natural Resources, Manitoba

Nutria
Greg Linscombe and Noel Kinler — Department of Fisheries and Wildlife, Louisiana

Coyote
F. Robert Henderson — Kansas State University, Kansas
Richard R. P. Stardom — Department of Natural Resources, Manitoba

Gray Wolf
Richard R. P. Stardom — Department of Natural Resources, Manitoba

Arctic Fox
Barry P. Saunders — Ministry of Environment, British Columbia

Red Fox
Kent E. Klepinger and Ned Norton — Department of Natural Resources, Wisconsin
Richard R. P. Stardom — Department of Natural Resources, Manitoba

Gray Fox
Ronald D. Andrews — Iowa Conservation Commission, Iowa

Brown Bear
Major L. Boddicker — Colorado State University, Colorado

Black Bear
Kent E. Klepinger and Ned Norton — Department of Natural Resources, Wisconsin

Polar Bear
Richard R. P. Stardom — Department of Natural Resources, Manitoba

Bassarisk
Norma Ames — Department of Game and Fish, New Mexico

Raccoon
Gary Schaffer — University of Georgia, Georgia
Randall L. Dibblee — P.E.I. Fish and Wildlife Division, Prince Edward Island

Marten
Barry P. Saunders — Ministry of Environment, British Columbia

Fisher
Chet McCord — Division of Fish and Wildlife, Massachusetts
Barry P. Saunders — Ministry of Environment, British Columbia

Short-tailed Weasel
F. Robert Henderson — Kansas State University, Kansas
Richard R. P. Stardom — Department of Natural Resources, Manitoba

Long-tailed Weasel
F. Robert Henderson — Kansas State University, Kansas
Richard R. P. Stardom — Department of Natural Resources, Manitoba

Mink
Noel Kinler and Greg Linscombe — Department of Fisheries and Wildlife, Louisiana
Barry P. Saunders — Ministry of Environment, British Columbia

Wolverine
Barry P. Saunders — Ministry of Environment, British Columbia

Badger
Ronald D. Andrews — Iowa Conservation Commission, Iowa

Striped Skunk
Charles L. Johnston — Arkansas Game and Fish Commission, Arkansas

Spotted Skunk
Ronald D. Andrews — Iowa Conservation Commission, Iowa

River Otter
Edward P. Hill — Mississippi Cooperative Fish and Wildlife Research Unit, U.S.F.W.S., Mississippi State University, Mississippi
Richard R. P. Stardom — Department of Natural Resources, Manitoba

Cougar
Charles L. Johnston — Arkansas Game and Fish Commission, Arkansas
Barry P. Saunders — Ministry of Environment, British Columbia

Lynx
Major L. Boddicker — Colorado State University, Colorado
Barry P. Saunders — Ministry of Environment, British Columbia

Bobcat
S. Douglas Miller — National Wildlife Federation, Washington, D.C.
Edward P. Hill — Mississippi Cooperative Fish and Wildlife Research Unit, U.S.F.W.S., Mississippi State University, Mississippi
Michael S. O'Brien — Nova Scotia Department of Lands and Forests, Wildlife Division, Nova Scotia

Northern Fur Seal
William P. Jensen, Jr. — Department of Natural Resources, Maryland

Harp Seal

W. Donald Bowen— Fisheries and Oceans, Newfoundland

Hooded Seal

W. Donald Bowen — Fisheries and Oceans, Newfoundland

Thanks go to the following state and provincial wildlife managers for providing the data on the status, management and range of furbearers in their respective states or provinces:

ALABAMA — Keith Guyse and Edward P. Hill; ALASKA — Robert A. Hinman and Herb R. Melchoir; ARIZONA — John Phelps; ARKANSAS — Lew Johnston; CALIFORNIA — Gordon I. Gould, Jr.; COLORADO — Harvey S. Donoho; CONNECTICUT — Joseph Risigo; DELAWARE — Lloyd Alexander and Tom Whittendale; FLORIDA — James R. Brady; GEORGIA — Dan Marshall; IDAHO — Ken Norrie and Roger Williams; ILLINOIS — George Hubert, Jr.; INDIANA — Larry E. Lehman; IOWA — Ron Andrews; KANSAS — Neil Johnson; KENTUCKY — Jim Durell; LOUISIANA — Greg Linscombe; MAINE — John H. Hunt; MARYLAND — Jim DiStefano; MASSACHUSETTS — James E. Cardoza; MICHIGAN — John Stuht and Joe Vogt; MINNESOTA — Blair Joselyn; MISSISSIPPI — Bill Hamrick; MISSOURI — David W. Erickson; MONTANA — Howard S. Hash; NEBRASKA — George Schildman and Bill Bailey; NEVADA — Stan J. Stiver and William A. Molini; NEW HAMPSHIRE — Forest Fogg; NEW JERSEY — Pat McConnell and Steve Toth; NEW MEXICO — George Merrill and Elizabeth McLellan; NEW YORK — Gary R. Parsons; NORTH CAROLINA — Randall C. Wilson; NORTH DAKOTA — Steve Allen; OHIO — Karl E. Bednarik; OKLAHOMA — Richard Hatcher; OREGON — Ralph R. Denney; PENNSYLVANIA — Arnold H. Hayden; RHODE ISLAND — Michael L. Lapisky; SOUTH CAROLINA — Derrell Shipes; SOUTH DAKOTA — Ron Fowler and Larry Frederickson; TENNESSEE — Gary W. Cook; TEXAS — Dan Boone and Joe T. Stevens; UTAH — Albert W. Heggen and Al Regenthal; VERMONT — Ben Day and Walt Cottrell; VIRGINIA — Dennis Martin; WASHINGTON — Mike Thorniley; WEST VIRGINIA — James R. Hill; WISCONSIN — Charles M. Pils and Kent Klepinger; WYOMING — Harry Harju; CANADA: ALBERTA — Arlen Todd; BRITISH COLUMBIA — Barry Saunders; MANITOBA — Dick Stardom; NEW BRUNSWICK — David J. Cartwright; NEWFOUNDLAND — Wallace R. Skinner; NORTHWEST TERRITORIES — Bruce Stephenson and N.M. Simmons; NOVA SCOTIA — Neil van Nostrand; ONTARIO — Milan Novak; PRINCE EDWARD ISLAND — Randall Dibblee; QUEBEC — Normand Traversy; SASKATCHEWAN — R. R. MacLennan; YUKON — Harvey Jessup.

Thanks go to Veronica Nicholls who typed the manuscript, Susan Morgan who proofread the entire book and Tom Cofield for proofreading the first draft of the species sections.

Special recognition goes to Capital-Gazette Publications, Inc. (Annapolis, Maryland) for their superior typesetting, Mobium Corporation for Design and Communication (Chicago, Illinois) for their excellent illustration work, Leonard Lee Rue III (Blairstown, New Jersey) for his quality photographs, R. R. Donnelly & Sons, Inc. (Chicago, Illinois) for the fine printing job and the League for the Handicapped, Inc. (Baltimore, Maryland) for their efficient and professional operation as our book distribution center.

CONTENTS

PREFACE

In 1975 the International Association of Fish and Wildlife Agencies (then known as the International Association of Game, Fish and Conservation Commissioners) formed a fur resources ad hoc committee to help those defending our rights to manage the furbearer resources from those who wanted all management to cease.

The objectives of this ad hoc committee, that received full committee status in 1976, were as follows:

(1) Assimilate and evaluate information relative to the status of furbearing animals. This information will include both biological and economic data, sociological aspects, and the status of all trap and trapping system research and appraisal.

(2) Develop and disseminate information to prove and promote the value of trapping systems as essential techniques for sound, scientific wildlife management in North America.

(3) Provide direction and coordination for future trapping techniques research and promote the continuance of efforts to develop and implement the most desirable systems.

(4) Annually report the status of anti-trapping issues in North America.

(5) Coordinate this committee's activities with appropriate committees of the International.

(6) Assist the International in the development of policy statements and programs essential to the management of wild fur resources of North America.

Since 1975 the Fur Resources Committee has made monumental strides in the publishing of data and information, helpful in the research and management of furbearers and vitally necessary with which to defend our management techniques and philosophies in a time of great controversy.

The committee annual reports, resource status reports, and book, "North American Furbearers, Their Research, Management and Harvest Status in 1976," continue to provide the world with information unobtainable anywhere.

The Fur Resources Committee also took the lead in the organization of the first Worldwide Furbearer Conference, which was held August 3-11, 1980. The resulting proceedings, published in three volumes, represented the cumulative knowledge of millions of dollars of research conducted in many countries.

The Fur Resources Committee is now pleased to publish this new reference, which we believe is the most complete general reference on North American furbearers in existence.

The committee will continue to assimilate and disseminate information in its efforts to meet the needs of wildlife managers and the resource.

Greg Linscombe
Chairman
Fur Resources Committee

FOREWORD

The past decade has seen great advancements in the fields of furbearer research and management. A vast amount of information is accumulating and the cooperative efforts of all the state and Canadian wildlife management agencies and the Fur Resources Committee of the International Association of Fish and Wildlife Agencies have resulted in the publication and international dissemination of defensible and objective harvest data, research and management information.

The first Worldwide Furbearer Conference was held August 3-11, 1980. This week-long conference had 200 attendees, representing twenty countries. The proceedings were published in three volumes and distributed internationally.

This book is another milestone in the dissemination of furbearer information.

It is efforts like those mentioned above which aid the true wildlife managers in the proper management, utilization and protection of our furbearer resources. Knowledge is the key to proper management of our natural resources.

Jack H. Berryman
Executive Vice President

INTRODUCTION

The word "fur" is derived from the old Germanic expression "forre", meaning sheath or scabbard. Apparently wild animals' skins were used for sheaths in the early days of European history, since sheepskins were used for clothing in that period.

Today, a "fur pelt" is defined in the commerce vernacular as an animal skin with all or part of the guard hair and/or fur fibers intact, which is used as an item of apparel for warmth or adornment. Nearly 100 types of animal pelts are utilized in fur trade.

Most fur pelts consist of skin, guard hairs and fur fibers. Guard hairs are long, glossy, strong, elastic hairs that overlie the shorter, soft, and duller fur fibers.

On the living animal, the function of guard hair is primarily one of protection from paludal and atmospheric moisture, while the function of fur fibers is to insulate the skin, especially in cold seasons or climates.

The relative values of fur pelts are dictated by their availability, color, completeness of guard hairs and fur fibers, size and contemporary fashion.

Historically, red and light colored furs were in demand because most furs were used as linings which contrasted stylishly with dark garment materials. Darker furs became more fashionable by the turn of the twentieth century as they were used as outside garment materials.

While wild fur-bearing animals are found in most countries, the United States and Russia produce the largest annual crops and the combined values of the U.S. and Canada's annual fur harvest make the North American wild fur industry the most valuable known in the world.

This book discusses the management, controversy and economic values associated with wild furbearers, and it details the general status of 30 of North America's major terrestrial, semi-aquatic and aquatic furbearers.

Several North American furbearers are not discussed in the species section of this reference because of their relatively small ranges, limited harvests or small economic impact in the wild fur industry. These furbearers are the red squirrel (*Tamiasciurus hudsonicus*), snowshoe hare (*Lepus americanus*), hog nose skunk (*Conepatus mesoleucus*), hooded skunk (*Mephitis macroura*), jack rabbit (*Lepus townsendii*), swift fox (*Vulpes macrotis*), and kit fox (*Vulpes velox*).

In recent years the combined harvest values of these furbearers has exceeded several million dollars. In some locales, the harvest of these species, especially squirrels and foxes, provides a significant income or service to residents of rural communities.

1

MANAGEMENT

Furbearer management is most often defined as the "wise use of a wildlife resource". The word "wise" in the definition cannot be defined until the aim of management is decided. It is the "aim of management" that sometimes makes management controversial. Simply stated, management is an attempt either to maintain conditions in a population of animals or to change conditions in the population to some particular desired situation.

Because of the dynamic conditions inherent in most furbearer populations and their habitats, management is generally a series of adjustments and monitoring programs.

The fact that most furbearers generally are harvested by trapping rather than hunting methods is due to their furtive nature. This characteristic makes observation and, therefore, the collection of data on these animals relatively difficult, thus adding to the complexity of management.

When the ecology (that branch of science concerned with the interrelationship of living things and their environment) of wildlife species is understood, it is obvious why some animals that were never hunted or trapped extensively became extinct, while others that have been hunted or trapped intensively are abundant. Land use is the controlling factor. The general status of any wildlife species is directly related to human use of the land.

Most of us realize that urbanization, industrialization and technology have altered and destroyed much of the natural environment, but few understand the ecology of the remaining wildlife populations. The drastic reductions and elimination of some species have greatly increased the population growth potentials of others.

Without human intervention some wildlife populations could grow to proportions that would be environmentally damaging. For example, the ecological impact resulting from high density and off-site furbearer populations could result in significant increases in diseases, agricultural depredation, and deterioration of their habitats.

Rabies and mange, tularemia, distemper and encephalitis are diseases commonly associated with high densities of coyotes and foxes, skunks, muskrats and raccoons respectively.

Coyotes, wolves and bobcats prey on domestic livestock; raccoons, muskrats and nutria eat agricultural crops; muskrats and beaver undermine roads and fields; muskrats tunnel through pond fills; muskrats and nutria create "eat-outs" (extensive mud flats) in marshes; beaver destroy fruit trees and ornamental vegetation, flood timber and crop lands and impair trout stream management programs in many areas; foxes and bobcats prey on poultry and other small livestock; otters are nuisances in fish ponds, especially brood fish ponds; and coyotes, raccoons, opossums and skunks are extreme nuisances in many suburban areas. In many semi-urban areas, particularly in the west, coyote attacks on domestic pets and humans are rising dramatically.

In addition to the problems discussed above, some furbearers can negatively affect other wildlife populations. For instance in some areas raccoon depredations of waterfowl, wild turkey, and sea turtle eggs have limited the reproductive success of these species.

If muskrat and/or nutria densities become too high in local situations "eat outs" often occur. An "eat out" describes a situation in a pond or marsh where these furbearers

2

have eaten completely the existing aquatic vegetation including the root systems which bind the organic soils together. This converts a marsh to a mucky area and sometimes destroys waterfowl, fish and other wetland wildlife habitat.

The population status of each of the nation's furbearers is directly related to the quantity and quality of their habitats. In fact, habitat degradation and destruction relative to urban expansion and industrial development are the only actual threats to the future conservation of the nation's wild furbearers.

In time, any over-population of an animal species will be reduced by either disease and parasitism, starvation, high population stress, or combinations of these. Without desirable systems of control, some animal populations would fluctuate from extreme highs to extreme lows, adversely affecting other plant and animal communities.

The relationship between birth and death rates determines whether a population decreases, stabilizes or increases in a given habitat. Man with his guns, steel traps, automobiles and mobile machinery is a predator of wild animals, and he can directly affect their population levels.

Seasonal harvests or killing of furbearers by hunters and trappers is desirable if it enhances the proper balance of birth and death rates. Regulated wildlife harvests are usually desirable and often necessary.

State and federal wildlife agencies monitor the effects of habitat changes and wildlife harvests. These agencies attempt to negotiate desirable systems of checks and balances in the natural environment by regulating the activities of hunters, trappers, fishermen, other outdoor recreationists and industrialists. Regulations are usually effective when they are supported and followed. Some individuals violate them.

Illegal, inhumane and destructive acts have been committed by some outdoor recreationists. Hunters have killed out of season, ignored the legal harvest limits and destroyed private property; fishermen have ignored the legal regulations, littered and polluted streams and have, also, destroyed private property; campers, hikers and picnickers have defaced, littered, polluted and burned untold acres of the natural landscape; and some people have caused unnecessary sufferings of captured wild creatures. Acts of despoilation are not common to any particular form of outdoor recreation, but are common to the activities of some "human animals".

These despoilers should never be confused with the desirable, beneficial and sporting outdoor recreationists. Those who desire humane treatment of wild animals are obviously interested in promoting their welfare and maintaining a "good life" for them. This is an admirable goal and one that is staunchly pursued by wildlifers and other students of ecology.

The composition and condition of wildlife populations are environmental barometers for man, because the basic life support systems which are necessary for wildlife are also essential to man's survival.

Are legal steel-trapping techniques inhumane? Inhumane treatment is usually defined as abnormally cruel or brutal treatment. An evaluation of cruelty and brutality with regard to wild animals is relative and must be made with an understanding of the instances in which these animals ultimately die. These circumstances include: being killed by predatory birds, mammals and reptiles; death from disease or parasitism, starvation, exposure or combinations of them; drowning; and being killed by automobiles or other mobile machinery.

If a wild animal is alert, fit and lucky enough to reach old age for its kind, it will undoubtedly become weakened by injuries, diseases, or other afflictions and become susceptible to predators or die slowly from starvation and exposure.

Steel-trapped animals may encounter several types of treatment and death. Trap sets for aquatic and semi-aquatic mammals (otter, beaver, muskrat, mink and raccoon) usually involve a leg-hold trap in a drowning technique or are killer traps. An animal caught in a "drowning set" is usually drowned within minutes after the trap snaps. Killer traps operate the same as the common mouse trap, in that they clamp across the animal's body. The killer trap is not an alternative to the leg-hold trap. Trap sites for leg-hold trap sets are not suitable for killer traps. The specific situations in which killer traps can be safely used are quite limited when compared with leg-hold trap sites. Also, non-target animals cannot be released alive from killer traps.

Terrestrial mammals like the coyote, fox, bobcat, skunk, fisher, opossum and weasel are normally caught at night in leg-hold trap sets. Depending on the nature and conditions of the trap set, the severity of the weather and the health of the captured animal, it may escape, die of exposure, or be killed by the trapper.

Are leg-hold traps brutal? Injuries sustained by animals caught in steel trap vary from slight bruises to lacerations, broken bones and amputated limbs. Each condition depends on the size of the trap, the nature of the trap set, the type of animal caught and the time interval between the trapper visits.

Illegal, irresponsible and thoughtless steel-trap uses can cause needless traumas in captured animals, but severe traumas for captured wild animals is not inherent in the use of steel traps.

Urbanization, which has removed most of the citizenry from the natural world, has created a barrier to the knowledge and understanding of the basic principals of ecology. In too many cases, an individual's knowledge of wildlife and the natural environment has been gleaned from staged and scripted wildlife movies and television programs. These programs are always colorful and entertaining, but seldom objective and educational. Many wildlife programs have been presented to the viewers in an anthropomorphic manner. Anthropomorphism is the act of ascribing human feelings, thoughts and actions to things which are not human. Those who tend to humanize wild animals and their living habits are being fanciful and unrealistic. Conversely, many so-called sportsmen's movies and TV programs have staged unsporting killing scenes which blatantly degrade hunting and trapping.

Opponents of steel traps often ask, "How would you like to be caught in a steel trap"? Obviously, we wouldn't, neither would we enjoy living like a wild animal or dying like one.

From a human point of view, these wild animals live and die in a degree of violence and pain that is only occasionally experienced by man — in warfare and some diseases.

If the emotional attitude, which is an abhorrence of steel-trapping because it hurts or kills animals, were followed to a restrictive conclusion, we could conceivably eliminate all forms of hunting and fishing, use of pesticides, even butchering of farm animals, because in all cases the animal is being "hurt" and usually killed. This unrealistic attitude is common to those who have learned to view the natural world anthropomorphically instead of clearly and objectively.

The natural death of any individual furbearer may be quick and violent or slow and torturing. Steel-trapped animals encounter deaths that are no more or less severe

4

than when they die naturally. Steel traps, when skillfully used, can cause less painful and protracted deaths than those to which the animals would otherwise succumb.

Steel-trapping is the most efficient, effective and desirable method known for harvesting, containing or reducing furbearer populations. The alternative methods of shooting, poisoning, gassing, habitat destruction and other trapping methods are usually either ineffective, economically prohibitive, non-selective (injurious to other animal populations, both wild and domestic), or dangerous to man.

Furbearer management programs, particularly regulated trapping programs, provide important incomes and meats to many rural families, and these furbearer harvests mitigate the potential for depredations and serious disease out-breaks.

Today's professional wildlife managers, agriculturalists and sportsmen realize that progressive furbearer management-harvesting programs are in fact wise uses of some of the continent's most valuable renewable wildlife resources.

Table 1.   **Furbearers extirpated from North American States/Provinces.**

SPECIES		STATES/PROVINCES WHERE EXTIRPATED*	CAUSES
Beaver	U.S.	CT, DE, IL, MD, NC, PA, RI, SC, WV	Habitat destruction and overharvest
	Canada	PI	
Black Bear	U.S.	IA, IL, KY, ND, NE, OH, RI, SD, CT, IN	Habitat destruction and overharvest
	Canada	PI	
Brown Bear	U.S.	CA, CO	Habitat destruction and shooting campaign
Cougar	U.S.	IL, IN, KY, MA, MD, MI, MO, NC, ND, NE, NH, NY, OH, PA, RI, SC, SD, TN, VA, VT, WI, WV	Habitat destruction and overharvest
	Canada	QU	
Fisher	U.S.	CT, ID, IL, IN, MD, MI, ND, PA, SD, UT, WI, WV	Habitat destruction
	Canada	NS, PI	
Lynx	U.S.	MA, ND, NE, NY, SD	Habitat destruction
	Canada	PI	
Marten	U.S.	IL, MA, MI, ND, NH, OH, PA, SD, VT, WI	Habitat destruction
	Canada	PI	
Swift Fox	U.S.	ND	Overharvest, traps, guns, poisons, poison campaign
	Canada	AL, MA	
River Otter	U.S.	IN, KS, KY, ND, NE, OK, WV, SD	Habitat destruction and overharvest
	Canada	PI	
Sea Otter	U.S.	OR	Overharvesting
	Canada	BC	
Spotted Skunk	U.S.	IN	Habitat destruction

6

Table 1. (Continued)

SPECIES		STATES/PROVINCES WHERE EXTIRPATED*	CAUSES
Gray Wolf	U.S.	AL, AZ, CO, CT, IL, IN, KS, KY, MA, MD, NO, ND, NE, NH, NY, OH, OR, PA, RI, SC, SD, TX, VA, WV	Habitat destruction and predator control
	Canada	NB, NF (Island Only)	
Red Wolf	U.S.	IN	Habitat destruction
Wolverine	U.S.	IA, MA, MI, PA, UT, WI	Habitat destruction
	Canada	NB	

*LIST OF STATE, PROVINCIAL AND TERRITORIAL ABBREVIATION CODES

UNITED STATES

Alabama	AL	North Carolina	NC
Alaska	AK	North Dakota	ND
Arizona	AZ	Ohio	OH
Arkansas	AR	Oklahoma	OK
California	CA	Oregon	OR
Colorado	CO	Pennsylvania	PA
Connecticut	CT	Rhode Island	RI
Delaware	DE	South Carolina	SC
District of Columbia	DC	South Dakota	SD
Florida	FL	Tennessee	TN
Georgia	GA	Texas	TX
Hawaii	HI	Utah	UT
Idaho	ID	Vermont	VT
Illinois	IL	Virginia	VA
Indiana	IN	Washington	WA
Iowa	IA	West Virginia	WV
Kansas	KS	Wisconsin	WI
Kentucky	KY	Wyoming	WY
Louisiana	LA		
Maine	ME	CANADA	
Maryland	MD		
Massachusetts	MA	Alberta	AL
Michigan	MI	British Columbia	BC
Minnesota	MN	Manitoba	MA
Mississippi	MS	New Brunswick	NB
Missouri	MO	Newfoundland	NF
Montana	MT	Northwest Territory	NT
Nebraska	NE	Nova Scotia	NS
Nevada	NV	Ontario	ON
New Hampshire	NH	Prince Edward Island	PI
New Jersey	NJ	Quebec	QU
New Mexico	NM	Saskatchewan	SK
New York	NY	Yukon Territory	YT

Table 2. **Furbearers introduced in North American States/Provinces.**

SPECIES	STATES/PROVINCES WHERE INTRODUCED		NATIVE OR EXOTIC	INTRODUCER	REASONS	RESULTS
Black Bear	U.S.	Kentucky	Native	Game & Fish Division	Sport hunting	Low populations
Beaver	U.S.	Alabama	"	Game & Fish Division	Extirpated furbearer	Viable populations
		Connecticut	"	Fisheries & Game Board	Water conservation	Viable populations
		Delaware	"	Maryland	Range expansion	"
		Florida	"	Georgia & Alabama	"	"
		Georgia	"	Unknown	Unknown	"
		Illinois	"	Conservation Department	Extirpated furbearer	"
		Indiana	"	"	"	"
		Kansas	"	Fish & Game Commission	Range expansion, aesthetics	"
		Maryland	"	Conservation Department	Extirpated furbearer	"
		Missouri	"	"	"	"
		New Jersey	"	Fish & Game	"	"
		New York	"	Fish & Wildlife Division	"	"

Table 2. (Continued)

SPECIES		STATES/PROVINCES WHERE INTRODUCED	NATIVE OR EXOTIC	INTRODUCER	REASONS	RESULTS
Beaver (cont'd)	U.S.	North Carolina	Native	Wildlife Resources	Water conservation	Viable populations
		Ohio	"	Natural Resources Department	Extirpated furbearer	"
		Oklahoma	"	Wildlife Conservation Department	Boost low populations	"
		Pennsylvania	"	Game Commission	Extirpated furbearer	"
		Rhode Island	"	Massachusetts & Connecticut	Range expansion	"
		South Carolina	"	U.S. Fish & Wildlife Service	Unknown	"
		Virginia	"	Game Commission	Extirpated furbearer	"
		West Virginia	"	Wildlife Resource Division	Water conservation	"
	Canada	Ontario	"	Natural Resources Ministry	Boost low populations	"
		P.E. Island	"	Fish & Game Association	Extirpated furbearer	"
		Quebec	"	Wildlife Service	Boost low populations	"

9

Table 2. (Continued)

SPECIES	STATES/PROVINCES WHERE INTRODUCED		NATIVE OR EXOTIC	INTRODUCER	REASONS	RESULTS
Coyote	U.S.	Florida	Exotic	Hunters	Dog Hunting	Viable populations
		Georgia	"	Unknown	Unknown	Viable populations
		Kentucky	"	"	"	Expanding populations
		Maryland	"	"	"	No known populations
		Mississippi	"	"	"	Viable populations
		North Carolina	"	"	"	No known populations
		Ohio	"	"	"	Low populations
		Rhode Island	"	"	"	Unknown
		West Virginia	"	"	"	No known populations
		Virginia	"	"	"	Unknown
Fisher	U.S.	Idaho	Native	Fish & Game Department	Extirpated furbearer	Viable populations
		Maryland	"	West Virginia	Range expansion	Low populations
		Massachusetts	"	New Hampshire	Range expansion	Viable populations
		Michigan	"	U.S. Forest Service and Natural Resources Department	Extirpated furbearer	" "
		Montana	"	Montana Dept. of Fish, Wildlife & Parks	"	Low populations

Table 2. (Continued)

SPECIES	STATES/PROVINCES WHERE INTRODUCED	NATIVE OR EXOTIC	INTRODUCER	RESOURCES	RESULTS
Fisher (cont'd)	U.S. New York	Native	Fish & Wildlife	Range expansion	Still in process
	Oregon	"	Fish & Wildlife Dept.	Porcupine control	Viable populations
	Rhode Island	"	Unknown	Unknown	Unknown
	Vermont	"	Forest & Parks Department	Porcupine control	Viable populations
	West Virginia	"	Wildlife Resources Division	Extirpated furbearer	"
	Wisconsin	"	Natural Resources Department	"	"
	Canada Nova Scotia	"	Lands & Forests Department	Porcupine control	"
	Ontario	"	Natural Resources Ministry	Boost low populations; introduce to geographically isolated areas -- now in progress	"
Marten	U.S. New Hampshire	"	U.S. Forest Service	Extirpated furbearer	Unknown
	Wisconsin	"	Natural Resources Department	"	"

11

Table 2. (Continued)

SPECIES	STATES/PROVINCES WHERE INTRODUCED		NATIVE OR EXOTIC	INTRODUCER	RESOURCES	RESULTS
Marten (cont'd)	U.S.	Michigan	Native	U.S. Forest Service and Natural Resources Department	Extirpated furbearer	Low populations
	Canada	Ontario	"	Natural Resources Ministry	Boost low populations	Unknown populations
Mongoose	U.S.	Hawaii	Exotic	Sugar cane growers	Rat control	Viable populations
		Florida	"	Containerized shipping	Accidental	Exterminated
Nutria	U.S.	Alabama	"	Conservation Department	Accidental	Viable populations
		Arkansas	"	Louisiana	Range expansion	"
		California	"	Fur farmers	Fur resource	Exterminated
		Colorado	"	"	"	Low populations
		Florida	"	"	"	Viable populations
		Georgia	"	Unknown	Unknown	"
		Idaho	"	"	"	Low populations
		Indiana	"	Fur farmers	Fur resource	Exterminated
		Kansas	"	"	"	Unknown
		Kentucky	"	Game & Fish Division	"	Did not survive

Table 2. (Continued)

SPECIES	STATES/PROVINCES WHERE INTRODUCED	NATIVE OR EXOTIC	INTRODUCER	REASONS	RESULTS
Nutria (cont'd)	U.S.				
	Louisiana	Exotic	Fur farmers	Accidental release	Viable populations
	Maryland	"	"	Fur resource	"
	Michigan	"	"	Accidental release	Did not survive
	Minnesota	"	"	"	"
	Mississippi	"	Louisiana	Range expansion	Viable populations
	Missouri	"	Unknown	Unknown	Did not survive
	Nebraska	"	"	"	"
	New Mexico	"	Game & Fish Department	Fur resource	Low populations
	North Carolina	"	Unknown	Unknown	Viable populations
	Ohio	"	Fur farmers	Fur resource	Did not survive
	Oklahoma	"	Unknown	Unknown	Low populations
	Oregon	"	Fur farmers	Intentional release	Viable populations
	Texas	"	Unknown	To remove pond vegetation	"
	Utah	"	Fur farmers	Fur resource	Did not survive
	Virginia	"	North Carolina	Range expansion	Viable populations
	Washington	"	Fur farmers	Fur resource	"

13

Table 2. (Continued)

SPECIES	STATES/PROVINCES WHERE INTRODUCED		NATIVE OR EXOTIC	INTRODUCER	REASONS	RESULTS
Nutria (cont'd)	Canada	Manitoba	Exotic	Fur farmers	Accidental release	Did not survive
		Nova Scotia	"	"	"	"
		Ontario	"	"	Fur resource	Low populations
Opossum	U.S.	California	"	"	"	Viable populations
		Oregon	"	"	Unknown	"
		Washington	"	Unknown	"	"
Raccoon	U.S.	Alaska	"	Fur farmers	Fur resource	"
		Kansas	"	Fur hunters	Hunting	"
	Canada	P.E. Island	"	Fur farmers	Released from pens when market collapsed	"
		C.B. Island	"	"	Fur resource	"
Red Fox	U.S.	California	"	"	"	"
		Florida	"	Fox hunters	Hunting	"
		Texas	"	"	"	"
		Washington	"	Fur farmers	Intentional release	"
Sea Otter	U.S.	Oregon	Native	Wildlife Department	Extirpated furbearer	Low populations
		Washington	"	"	Aesthetic furbearer	"

Table 2. (Continued)

SPECIES	STATES/PROVINCES WHERE INTRODUCED		NATIVE OR EXOTIC	INTRODUCER	REASONS	RESULTS
Sea Otter (cont'd)	Canada	British Columbia	Native	Wildlife Department	Extirpated furbearer	Low populations
River Otter	U.S.	Colorado	"	"	"	" "
Striped Skunk	Canada	P.E. Island	Exotic	Fur farmers	Released from pens when market collapsed	Viable populations

Table 3. **North American States/Provinces paying for furbearer depredations.**

SPECIES	STATES/PROVINCES THAT PAY		TYPE OF DAMAGE
Bear	U.S.	Colorado	Livestock, apiary and orchard depredation
		Maine	
		New Hampshire	" "
		Pennsylvania	" "
		Vermont	" "
		West Virginia	" "
		Wisconsin	" "
		Wyoming	" "
	Canada	Alberta	Apiary depredation only
		Manitoba	" " "
		Ontario	" " "
		Quebec	" " "
		Saskatchewan	" " "
Cougar	U.S.	Colorado	Livestock depredation
		New Hampshire	" "
		Wyoming	" "
	Canada	Alberta	" "
Coyote	U.S.	Iowa	Livestock depredation
		Maine	" "
	Canada	Alberta	" "
		Ontario	" "
		Quebec	" "
Wolf	U.S.	Minnesota	Livestock depredation
	Canada	Alberta	" "
		Ontario	" "
		Quebec	" "

TRAPPING TECHNOLOGY

From the onset of the great North American "fur rush" in the late 1500s trappers have necessarily depended on snares and steel traps for capturing wild furbearers. Steel-jawed foot traps originally were introduced into North America from Europe but by the 18th century most steel traps were made by American blacksmiths.

Since the late 1800s scores of inventors have developed hundreds of new trap prototypes as well as modifications to previous designs. Many were patented but most proved to be unsuitable in actual field conditions.

The wild fur market was erratic and generally depressed in the early 1900s but a post World War II revival of market values for wild furbearers prompted a renewed interest in trapping technology. This interest was expanded by a growing number of new wildlife researchers and management scientists that viewed traps as tools of wildlife research and management programs.

Two significant innovations were the Aldrich bear snare (a spring-powered foot snare designed and developed specifically for capturing bears) and the Conibear trap (a spring-powered, body-gripping, kill trap). The Aldrich snare eliminated the need for the large and dangerous steel traps commonly referred to as "bear traps", and the use of Conibear traps revolutionized the capture methodology for semi-aquatic furbearers in some aquatic and wetland situations.

In recent years, trap manufacturing companies and private inventors have developed many new spring-powered traps including footsnares, body-gripping traps and steel-jawed legholds in new sizes and configurations. Other recent innovations include such modifications as offset jaws, padded jaws, tranquilizer tabs and pan tension devices. All recent innovations result from extensive efforts to increase efficiency of trapping systems by increasing the selectivity and/or reducing visible injury to trapped animals.

Today, trappers, trap manufacturers and wildlife professionals are expanding their field evaluation programs for the new experimental trapping devices. Modern trap research and development efforts are not expected to reveal any all-encompassing replacements for current trapping systems. They are expected to increase the efficiency and selectivity of capture techniques and reduce the frequency and degree of trap-related injuries to captured animals.

The state of the art of trap and furbearer harvest system evaluation and research is developing rapidly. There is a need to proceed rigorously in evaluation, but cautiously in implementation of new systems.

Trapping system evaluations and research should include, but not be limited to, a scientifically and statistically designed methodology followed by field evaluation under a variety of environmental, political, sociological and economic conditions that exist domestically, as well as internationally.

CONTROVERSY

For more than 60 years the management of wild fur-bearing animals has been steeped in controversy. National anti-trapping campaigns were intensively waged in the 1920s and again in the 1970s.

Opponents of steel-trapping operations are protectionists (certain animal welfare organizations) and some houndsmen (fox and raccoon hunters and fox chasers), while proponents of steel trap uses are professional wildlife managers, trappers and other sportsmen, all other sectors of the wild fur industry and agriculturalists.

The 1920s and 1970s were decades of intense political anti-trapping campaigns. In both cases, the trapping controversies followed on the heels of anti-seal killing campaigns that apparently stimulated a public resentment of the commercial use of wild animal pelts and, subsequently, the methods used for capturing furbearers.

By 1911, Alaska's North Pacific fur seal herd had been reduced to a low of about 250,000 animals, a small fraction of its former size. So the federal government negotiated an agreement among all countries that hunted North Pacific fur seals (Canada, Japan, Russia and the United States) to ban pelagic sealing and control the rookery harvests on Japan's Robben Islands, Russia's Commander Islands, and Alaska's Pribilof Islands. During that time, William Hornaday, then Director of the New York Zoological Park, fought to "save" the fur seals by lobbying Congress to stop the Pribilof hunts. Hornaday was not successful in his "seal-saving" campaign but he continued to espouse the simplistic notion that hunting alone was decimating wild animal populations. Accordingly, he developed the "Permanent Wildlife Protection Fund" with a budget of more than $100,000 to combat hunters, his alleged "enemies" of wildlife.

In 1915, Congress created the Bureau of the Biological Survey to manage Alaska's wildlife, regulate migratory bird hunting, and conduct control programs for such animals as wolves and bobcats.

Hornaday and the Wildlife Protection Fund crusaded against the new Bureau. The "anti-Bureau" crusade escalated in 1920 when former naval intelligence officer Commander Edward Breck founded the Anti-Steel-Trap-League in Washington, D.C. The League focused its campaign against the use of the "vicious" and "cruel" steel trap in animal damage control programs.

In 1925, the Anti-Steel-Trap-League changed its name to Defenders of Wildlife, but continued to distribute Anti-Steel-Trap-League brochures and circulars.

The trapping controversy bloomed in the late 1920s when fox and raccoon hunters spearheaded campaigns to outlaw steel traps in South Carolina and Georgia. Then in 1930, as a result of houndsmen and protectionist campaigns, Massachusetts banned leghold traps.

Then came the great depression of the 1930s and in light of desperate economic conditions, South Carolina, Georgia and Massachusetts rescinded their bans on steel traps.

Protectionism proliferated in the 1950s when new anti-hunting and trapping organizations such as the Animal Welfare Institute, Humane Society of the United States, and Friends of Animals were founded.

In the mid 1960s public resentment of the killing of seals was roused by the

Canadian Broadcasting Corporation's film "Artek", purportedly an expose' on Canada's harp seal hunt. The film depicted violent shooting and clubbing scenes and a scene of a hunter apparently skinning a live seal. Almost immediately, and worldwide, news commentaries began condemning the "clubbing of baby seals" (whitecoats), and the "Save the Seals" organization was founded to stop the harp seal hunt.

In response to public pressure, Canada's House of Commons held hearings on the harp seal hunt. The testimony exposed the inaccuracies and misrepresentations of protectionist propaganda campaigns as well as factual evidence that the seals were not threatened with extinction. Also, the hunter depicted in the "Artek" film confessed in a sworn affidavit that he had been paid by the film makers to "try and skin a seal alive" for the camera. He said they asked him "not to hit the seal first."

By that time the traditional method of killing rookery seals had become so controversial that the U.S. government commissioned 3 independent studies to determine the most humane method of killing seals. Studies were performed by representatives of the Humane Society of the United States, the National Academy of Sciences, the U.S. Department of Agriculture, the Bureaus of Sport Fisheries and Wildlife and Commercial Fisheries, the Virginia Mason Research Center, the American Veterinary Medical Association, and Batelle Columbus Laboratory. The researchers found that no other method was as humane as the traditional "stun and stick" method. Finally (in 1977), a U.S. federal court ruled that the traditional method of killing rookery fur seals was in fact humane.

In 1969 the Canadian Association for Humane Trapping (CAHT) claimed that a scientific study showed that 3 out of every 4 animals caught by trappers were unwanted and therefore discarded.

By 1970 the Fund for Animals and the Animal Protection Institute had been founded. They added significantly to the anti-hunting and trapping campaigns.

The trapping controversy exploded in the early 1970s. Florida's Game and Freshwater Fish Commission banned steel traps, then the Massachusetts legislature prohibited the upland use of leghold traps and New Jersey's legislature banned leghold traps in 11 of its 21 counties.

One of the most effective visual aids used in anti-trap campaigns was the CAHT's film "They Take So Long To Die", which showed gruesome scenes of animals struggling in traps. The film was made with animals that had been previously trapped in the wild then moved to a small compound where they were "trapped again" using bad techniques to depict inhumane conditions for the camera.

In 1973, Canada's federal and provincial governments formed the "Federal-Provincial-Committee-for-Humane-Trapping" to test all known traps for efficiency and humaneness, to encourage the development of more humane traps and trapping systems and to review all aspects of trapping in Canada.

The CAHT reacted in a positive manner by withdrawing their film "They Take So Long To Die" from circulation and supporting the new committee. The CAHT also explained that the study they cited, showing that 3 of every 4 trapped animals were unwanted, was an Ontario Lands and Forest experiment, using a variety of traps and lures including shiny objects that were attractive to birds and other non-target animals, and that the capture data were misleading because the researchers had apparently set 150 traps in an area that would normally accommodate only about 15 traps.

Every wildlife agency was affected in 1974 when scores of anti-trapping bills were introduced in state legislatures and in Congress. By this time the states realized that the trapping issue was simply the tip of the anti-hunting iceberg.

In 1975, Congress held hearings on several anti-trap bills. Mary Tyler Moore and Cleveland Amory led the host of protectionist witnesses. They showed scenes from "They Took So Long To Die" and Ms. Moore cried in front of the television cameras. But testimony from wildlife managers, trappers and other opponents of the legislation was well received and the bills were buried.

In 1977, all North American wildlife agencies watched the Ohio anti-trapping referendum campaign closely. It was well known that referendum ballots were protectionists' greatest hope for reform. Pro-trapping and anti-trapping forces spent nearly half a million dollars in their efforts and when it was over the pro-trapping forces had won by a 2 to 1 margin. The protectionists regrouped, blamed their loss on the low voter turnout (in an off-year election) and promised success in future referenda.

In 1978, Rhode Island's legislature banned the use of leghold traps.

In 1980, Oregon's anti-trapping referendum was also defeated by a 2 to 1 margin.

And in 1981, Canada's Federal-Provincial-Committee-for-Humane-Trapping printed its final report. Even though the opportunities for using kill-trapping systems are far greater in Canada than in the U.S., the report recognizes the fact that leg-holding trapping systems are essential for capturing wild canids (i.e. foxes, coyotes and wolves).

In the U.S. today, leg-holding trapping techniques are essential to the population control and harvest of virtually every species of wild fur-bearing mammal in every State.

RANCHED FUR

North America is a significant producer of domestic fur — fox, mink, and chinchilla. The farming and production of these species have undergone tremendous changes in recent years. The liquidation of the silver fox industry in the early 1940s prompted the expansion of mink farming and simultaneously the chinchilla pelt market was developed.

FOX

Fox farming is primarily concerned with the production of "silver" and "blue" fox pelts which are color variations of the red fox and arctic fox, respectively. The world's first domestically bred silver fox occurred on Prince Edward Island, Canada in 1894.

By 1940 the annual world production of silver fox furs had reached 1,000,000 pelts. The major producers were the U.S., Canada and Scandinavia, respectively. But by 1953, the annual silver fox pelt crop had dropped to 250,000 and by 1955 only 8,000 pelts were produced. The silver fox farmers turned to mink production.

In 1963 the Japanese exhibited a moderate interest in silver fox pelts and by the late 1960s Japan became a major market for fox pelts. Long-hired furs became universally fashionable in the early 1970s and this demand prompted new growth in fox farming.

MINK

In 1966, the annual North American mink farm production (11,000,000 pelts) accounted for one half of the annual world mink farm production. But by the early 1970s, North America's mink farm production had decreased by 65 percent. The increased world supply of "ranch mink", coupled with low production costs in Russia and Europe, were the primary causes. But the farm mink industry was revived by 1970 when consumer demand for wild furs was spurred by the initial appearance of "fun furs". Today the U.S. annually produces about 3.3 million ranch mink while Canada produces about one million. In 1980 the worldwide production of ranched mink was approximately 28,000,000 skins.

Today the number of American mink ranches is increasing, since the sharp reduction in mink farming a decade ago. According to the crop report, there were 1,122 farms producing mink in the U.S. in 1980. Wisconsin is still the leader with 267 ranches, followed by Utah with 190, and Minnesota with 158. That year, Wisconsin produced 997,000 ranched mink pelts, Utah produced 465,700, and Minnesota marketed 442,900 ranched mink pelts.

CHINCHILLA

Chinchilla farming began in California in the 1920s when Mathias Chapman imported several chinchillas that were trapped in the upper regions of the Andes in South America. The early chinchilla markets were for breeding pairs (not pelts) which were sold to prospective fur farmers. The actual chinchilla pelt market was developed after the demand for live animals had waned. The North American 1981 chinchilla crop was estimated at 150,000 pelts. The largest producers are the U.S. and Canada, followed by Europe, Japan and South America.

ECONOMIC VALUES

The economic values of furbearers transcend the income derived by fur harvesters for fur. There is a "benefits chain" (see Fig. 1) which involves hundreds of thousands of people and billions of dollars.

Furbearers are a unique resource and their mere existence or absence has economic impact.

While figures are not readily available for the economic values of furbearer management to landowners, farmers and local commerce, it is known that the harvesting and management of furbearers has an economic impact of hundreds of millons of dollars in North America annually.

Timber loss and crop depredation due to overpopulation of beaver have cost the southeastern agricultural community in excess of $264 million over the past ten years. Livestock losses due to coyote depredation in the sixteen western states during 1978 cost producers $25.4 million. These losses do not include any indirect or multiplier impact such as additional cost to consumers resulting from reduced supplies due to depredation. There are numerous examples of losses that landowners incur when furbearer populations are not prudently managed. If there was no management these losses would greatly increase, as would costs for controlling diseases and nuisance animals.

The entire carcass of each furbearer has economic value.

The furbearers provide many commodities in addition to fur pelts. The body parts of fur-bearing animals are used in many ways; meats are used as food items; scent glands and urine are used by the lure industry; glandular substances are used by the perfume industry; glands and baccula are used by the aphrodisiac industry; and skins, bones, teeth, and claws are used in the wildlife art and jewelry industries. The specific economic values for these products are not presently available, but some states maintain furbearer meat sales records.

Louisiana's meat harvest for the 1979-80 season was as follows:

Species	No. of Pounds	Price/lb.	Value
Nutria	582,000	.04	$ 23,280.00
Muskrat	18,000	.04	720.00
Raccoon	930,000	.30	279,000.00
Opossum	95,000	.25	23,750.00
TOTAL	1,625,000		$326,750.00

The value of North America's wild fur pelt harvest is conservatively estimated to be over 500 million dollars annually. The U.S. produces the most muskrat, raccoon, bobcat, red fox, badger, otter, skunk, coyote, and mink pelts; while Canada produces the most beaver, fisher, arctic fox, lynx, marten, red squirrel, and ermine pelts. The gray fox, nutria, opossum and bassarisk are essentially U.S. species.

The average prices for each furbearer vary considerably in each region of North America but, generally speaking, the U.S. presently receives higher average pelt prices for the wolf, bobcat, raccoon, and muskrat, while Canada receives higher average pelt prices for the beaver, coyote, red fox, marten, mink and otter. The average prices for all other North American furbearers are essentially the same in both countries.

Pelt prices are controlled by demand which is primarily controlled by availability, durability, and fashion. The simple law of supply and demand is complicated by many factors in the world's fur industry. One factor is the use of raw fur as an international medium of exchange.

Generally speaking, fur pelts are money. They can be moved from place to place at will and sold at any fur auction or in private treaty sales. The usual system of buying and selling of furs for cash provides a vehicle for investors to convert their money to a readily convertible commodity during times of economic crises, such as drastic changes in the value of a nation's currency or the international market. Therefore, fur sales must be viewed as money movers as well as commodity sales.

A furbearer is worth not just X dollars, but rather a relative value to other furbearers (X muskrats, X beaver, X raccoons, X foxes, etc.). Since a fur harvester will strive to maximize his economic return, he will take those pelts which afford the greatest monetary return for his time and effort. Although many hunters and trappers pursue the same species each year, the total harvest effort is greatly directed by ambient prices. Consquently, changes in the average pelt prices for a given species may not affect the harvest presures on it if its relative value when compared to other furbearers doesn't change.

Other factors may influence the value of furbearer pelts, as exemplified by the effect on beaver pelt prices of the temporary closure of beaver processing plants in Milan, Italy in the early 1970s. Since the majority of the world's beaver pelts were processed in that city, the labor-management problems and resultant production slow-down thwarted the movement of beaver pelts and prices dropped even though the demand for beaver fur garments was strong. By the mid-1970s the processing plants had closed and beaver pelt prices dropped to their lowest average in many years. The processing plants returned to full production in 1977 and beaver pelt prices escalated to their normal expected level.

North America's wild furbearer pelts and meats have sold for more than 500 million dollars annually in recent years, while ranched fur pelts have grossed more than 100 million dollars annually.

Considering inflationary trends and the additional uses of furbearer products, it is probable that North America's fur-bearing animals will become a one billion dollar industry at the production (farming, hunting, and trapping) level within the foreseeable future.

Processed pelts are ultimately used in finished fur garments. The fur garment industry is in itself a billion dollar industry, which employs approximately 250,000 people in the U.S., either directly or indirectly. U.S. retail sales of furbearer garments in 1980 was $944 million while the wholesale exports of garments and pelts exceeded $552 million that same year.

Furs represent one of the few American consumer product industries that have a favorable balance of trade.

The U.S. exports fur garments and pelts to more than 30 countries throughout the world. West Germany, Japan and Switzerland are principal buyers.

U.S. Department of Commerce records indicate that in 1980 fur exports totalled $552 million, while fur imports totalled $310 million for the same period.

In summary, the total economic values of the United States and Canadian renewable wild furbearer resources cannot be fully appreciated without considering the damages that steel-trapping prevents annually, the wild furbearer harvest (furs, meats,

Fig. 1. Furbearer Resource Utilization Benefits Chain

RESOURCE
1. Manages population densities
2. Prevents diseases
3. Prevents eat outs or destruction of habitat
4. Removes annual surplus to maintain vigorous, healthy populations

PEOPLE
1. Reduces and prevents diseases
2. Manages populations to prevent nuisance animal situations
3. Aesthetic and practical appreciation of nature through observation, management and utilization

LANDOWNER
1. Reduces crop loss and damage
2. Reduces livestock and poultry losses
3. Reduces property damages
4. Reduces diseases

LOCAL ECONOMY
Businesses benefit from sale of gas, food, equipment and supplies

ACT OF HARVESTING A FURBEARER

STATE GOVERNMENT
1. Raises license fees for state wildlife management agencies
2. Raises income from lands leased for management
3. Manages wildlife populations and prevents diseases
4. Reduces nuisance complaints which state answers

HARVESTED FURBEARER

TRAPPER
1. Earns money from fur
2. Earns money from meat
3. Earns money from glands
4. Earns money from teeth and bones
5. Gains a source of food

STATE GOVERNMENT
1. Raises money from licenses and permits
2. Raises money from state and federal income taxes

24

BUSINESS
1. Benefits communications companies
2. Benefits transportation companies
3. Benefits insurance companies
4. Benefits garment retailers
5. Benefits retailers' employees
6. Benefits advertising agencies
7. Benefits publications through income from advertising

STATE AND FEDERAL GOVERNMENTS
1. Benefits state retail sales tax division
2. Benefits Internal Revenue Service

FINISHED GARMENT

FUR PELT

BUSINESS
1. Benefits raw fur pelt buyer
2. Benefits processed fur pelt buyer
3. Benefits investors
4. Benefits fur pelt processors
5. Benefits fashion designers
6. Benefits equipment manufacturers
7. Benefits insurance companies
8. Benefits communications companies
9. Benefits transportation companies
10. Benefits garment manufacturers

STATE AND FEDERAL GOVERNMENTS
1. Raises money for licenses to deal in furs
2. Raises money for income taxes (state and federal)

and other products), the revenues derived through state and federal licenses and taxes, and the many businesses involved in or associated with the fur pelt, fur garment and fur fashion industries.

REFERENCES
FOR INTRODUCTION, MANAGEMENT, TRAPPING TECHNOLOGY,CONTROVERSY, RANCHED FUR AND ECONOMIC VALUES

ALLEN, D.L. 1954. Our Wildlife Legacy. Funk and Wagnalls. New York. 422 pp.

ANONYMOUS. 1939. New Hope for the Biological Survey. National Anti-Steel Trap League. Washington, D.C. 31 pp.

_____. 1977. A Fact Sheet on Sealing. Canada Today. Ottawa, Ontario. 8(10): 1-12.

_____. 1979. Environmental Impact Statement on the Interim Convention on Conservation of North Pacific Fur Seals. U.S. Dept. Commerce. Washington, D.C. 136 pp.

DUNN, D.L. 1977. Canada's East Coast Sealing Industry in 1976. Canadian Fish and Marine Service. Ind. Rep. 98. Ottawa, Ontario. 54 pp.

PARKER, Sandy. Monthly. Sandy Parker Reports. Sandford Advertising, Inc. Box 497, Valley Stream, N.Y. 11580. 4 pp.

PURSLEY, D. 1973. The Great Steel-Trap Hassle. Wonderful West Virginia. West Virginia Department of Natural Resources. Charleston, West Virginia. Vol. 37, No. 8. 32 pp.

_____. 1981. An Update on the Wildlife Management Controversy. Trans. Northeast Sect. Wildl. Soc. 38: 51-68.

REIGER, G. 1978. Hunting and Trapping in the New World. H.P. Brokaw, Ed. Wildlife and America. U.S. Gov. Print. Off. Washington, D.C. 42-52 pp.

ROPPEL, A.Y. and S. P Davey. 1965. Evolution of Fur Seal Management on the Pribilof Islands. J. Wildl. Manage. 29: 448-463.

TREFETHEN, J.B. 1975. An American Crusade for Wildlife. Winchester Press. New York. 409 pp.

SPECIES SECTIONS

SECTION I
ORDER MARSUPALIA

OPOSSUM
(*Didelphis virginiana*)

DESCRIPTION: The opossum is a medium sized animal with long, coarse, grayish-white fur; a sharp pointed, slender muzzle; prominent, thin, naked ears; short legs; and a long, scaly, scantily haired, prehensile tail. Each front foot has 5 clawed toes, while each hind foot has 4 clawed toes and a divergent clawless, thumblike, grasping toe. Although gray is the most common color, other color phases exist. The pelage may be phases of brown or black and occasionally all white (albinos). Sexes are alike in appearance. Mature females have a prominent fur-lined pouch (marsupium) on their bellies. The pouch contains up to 17 mammae. Males are usually larger than females. Adults may attain a total length of 40 inches (102 cm) including a 9 to 20 inch (23-51 cm) tail and weigh up to 15 pounds (7 kg). The opossum is the ony native marsupial (pouched animal) in North America.

HABITAT: The opossum inhabits woodlands near or along streams, ponds, lakes, swamps and marshes. It prefers farmland and woodlots to extensively forested areas. Opossums utilize the den sites of other animals, cavities in rock piles, brush piles and trash heaps, hollow trees and logs, and buildings.

FEEDING HABITS: Opossums are opportunistic feeders. They eat a wide variety of food items but prefer animal matter during all seasons. Most flesh foods are carrion. Common food items are insects, reptiles, amphibians, birds and their eggs, crustaceans, worms, grubs, persimmons, berries and other fruits, and cereal grains.

BEHAVIOR: The opossum is shy, secretive and primarily nocturnal. It is commonly seen at night along highways feeding on traffic-killed animals. Opossums tend to be nomadic but a few individuals have exhibited fixed ranges in areas as small as 40 acres (16 ha) in size. Opossums are not aggressive. They readily retreat (when pursued by man or other animals) into trees, brush piles or other types of cover. When frightened, opossums bare their teeth and drool saliva. A common and well known defense mechanism is feigning death or "playing possum" when cornered. The animal lies on its side, closes its eyes, becomes limp and motionless; the mouth is open and the tongue hangs out. This involuntary reaction is caused by a brief nervous shock. The animal recovers quickly and usually attempts to escape. Opossums are usually inactive at temperatures below 20 degrees F, (-21 C) and they tend to "hole up" during severe winter weather. Opossums are solitary animals except during mating activities and when in winter shelters. They are well adapted for climbing and the grasping hind toe facilitates the opossums' ability to hang on to small branches. Opossums can hang head down supported by their hind feet and tails or solely by the prehensile tail for short periods of time. They are strong swimmers and will voluntarily enter water, especially in shallow areas.

REPRODUCTION: Most breeding occurs in the January through March period (February is the peak month) but litters can occur year round. Gestation is only 12 to 13 days. Litter sizes range from 5 to 13 (average is 9) and the young are blind and extremely altricial. The young appear to be tiny embryos with well formed claws on the front limbs which enable the newborn to crawl into the mother's pouch. The young are less than ⅓

33

inch (8.5 mm) in length and weigh approximately 1/175 ounce (0.14 g). After entering the pouch each newborn attaches itself to a teat and remains "locked" on to it for approximately 60 days. At about 80 days of age the young are fairly well developed and able to leave the pouch for short periods of time. The young opossums stay with their mother continuously for approximately 100 days. Opossums mature sexually and breed during their first year of life.

POPULATION STATUS: Opossums are among the most primitive of living mammals. They date back nearly to the dinosaur age. They have expanded their range northward in recent times and become more numerous. In northern portions of their range opossums frequently exhibit frostbitten ears and tails. Opossums are most abundant in the southern and eastern U.S. They are less abundant in the north and in the west, and their occurrence along the Pacific Coast results from introduction by man. The opossum's fecundity, adaptability and opportunistic feeding habits ensure its continued existence in viable populations through the foreseeable future.

UTILIZATION: The opossum is the most common furbearer in the southern woodlands. It is sought by both trappers and houndsmen. In the south, "possum" dishes, particularly baked opossum, are a delicacy to many people. The fur is widely used for trimmings and choice skins are used in the manufacture of whole coats. In recent years the harvest of opossum in the U.S. has exceeded 1 million pelts valued at more than 2.5 million dollars annually.

REFERENCES

GARNER, A.L. 1973. The Systematics of the Genus (*Didelphis*) in North and Middle America. Lubbock Texas Tech. Press. 81 pp.

HALL, E.R. 1981. The Mammals of North America. Vol. II. John Wiley & Sons, Inc., New York. 1181 pp.

HARTMAN, C.G. 1928. The Breeding Season of the Opossum (*Didelphis virginiana*) and the Rate of Intra-uterine and Postnatal Development. J. Morph. and Physiol. 46: 143-215.

_____. 1952. Possums. University of Texas Press. Austin. 174 pp.

KEEFE, F. 1967. The World of the Opossum. Philadelphia, Lippincott. 144 op.

LAY, D.W. 1942. Ecology of the Opossum in Eastern Texas. J. Mamma. 23: 147-159.

McCARDY, E. Jr. 1938. The Embryology of the Opossum. Am. Anatom. Memoris. 16: 233 pp.

PETRIDES. G.A. 1949. Sex and Age Determination in the Opossum. J. Mammal. 30: 364-378.

REYNOLDS, H.C. 1945. Some Aspects of the Life History and Ecology of the Opossum in Central Missouri. J. Mammal. 26: 361-379.

_____. 1952. Studies on Reproduction in the Opossum (*Didelphis virginiana virginiana*). Univ. of Calif. Public. in Zool. 52: 223-284.

SCHWARTZ, C.W., and E.R. Schwartz. 1964. The Wild Mammals of Missouri. Univ. of Missouri Press and Missouri Conservation Commission, Kansas City. 341 pp.

WISEMAN, G.L., and G.O. Hendrickson. 1950. Notes on the Life History and Ecology of the Opossum in Southeast Iowa. J. Mammal. 31: 331-337.

Map 1. The Range of the Opossum in the United States and Canada.

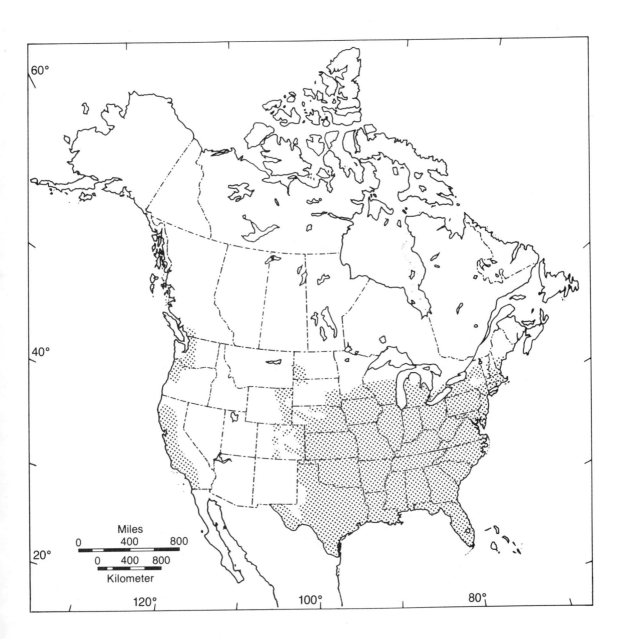

Fig. 1

The Management Status of the Opossum in the United States and Canada

STATES, PROVINCES AND TERRITORIES	Present	Total Protection	Hunting Season	Trapping Season	Year-Round Harvesting	Limited Harvesting	Food Resource	Habitat Management	Population Inventories	Special Regulations	Private Lands Leased
United States											
Alabama	●		●	●		●	●			●	
Alaska											
Arizona	●	●									
Arkansas	●		●	●		●	●				
California	●			●	●		●				
Colorado	●		●	●	●						
Connecticut	●		●	●		●	●			●	
Delaware	●			●			●				
Florida	●			●			●			●	
Georgia	●		●	●		●	●			●	
Idaho											
Illinois	●		●	●		●	●		●	●	
Indiana	●		●	●		●	●		●		
Iowa	●		●	●		●	●		●	●	
Kansas	●		●	●		●	●				
Kentucky	●		●	●		●					
Louisiana	●		●	●	●	●	●			●	
Maine	●			●		●					
Maryland	●		●	●		●				●	
Massachusetts	●		●	●		●					
Michigan	●			●			●				
Minnesota	●			●							
Mississippi	●		●	●		●	●			●	
Missouri	●		●	●		●	●		●	●	
Montana											
Nebraska	●		●	●		●	●			●	
Nevada											
New Hampshire	●			●							
New Jersey	●		●	●		●	●		●		
New Mexico											
New York	●			●							
North Carolina	●		●	●		●	●				●
United States (Cont'd)											
North Dakota											
Ohio	●		●	●			●				
Oklahoma	●		●	●		●			●		
Oregon	●			●	●						
Pennsylvania	●		●	●	●						
Rhode Island	●			●		●			●	●	
South Carolina	●		●	●		●	●		●		
South Dakota	●		●	●							
Tennessee	●		●	●		●					
Texas	●		●	●	●					●	
Utah											
Vermont	●				●						
Virginia	●		●	●			●		●		
Washington	●				●				●		
West Virginia	●		●	●	●	●					
Wisconsin	●		●	●	●						
Wyoming	●		●	●	●						
Total (United States)	42	1	28	33	18	23	23	0	8	14	1
Canada											
Alberta											
British Columbia	●	●									
Manitoba											
New Brunswick											
Newfoundland											
Northwest Territories											
Nova Scotia											
Ontario	●										
Prince Edward Island											
Quebec											
Saskatchewan											
Yukon Territory											
Total (Canada)	2	1	0	0	0	0	0	0	0	0	0

SECTION II
ORDER RODENTIA

BEAVER
(*Castor canadensis*)

DESCRIPTION: The beaver is semi-aquatic and the largest North American rodent with rich brown fur and a uniquely paddle-shaped tail. The scaled, hairless tail is used as a rudder when the beaver is swimming and as a prop when the animal is standing. The beaver's ears and nose have internal valves that close when it dives and its lips can close tightly behind its prominent incisors, enabling it to cut wood or peel bark under water. The large orange upper and lower incisors grow continuously but are worn down by the animal's tree cutting and feeding activities. These incisors wear more quickly on the back than the front so a sharp cutting edge is maintained. The beaver has a pair of large scent glands near the anus and a split second toenail on each hind foot which is used to comb the fur and spread the oil over the coat. Adults average 30 to 65 pounds (14-29 km) in weight and 25 to 30 inches (64-76 cm) in length. The tail usually is 9 to 10 inches (23-25 cm) long and about 6 inches (15 cm) wide on adults. Beavers are somewhat larger in more northerly latitudes. The sexes are indistinguishable in appearance (except for the swollen mammaries on nursing females) because both have a cloaca, a common opening for the reproductive organs, bladder and anus. The skull contains 20 teeth and there are 4 mammae.

HABITAT: The beaver inhabits slow-flowing forested and some agricultural waterways and wetlands throughout North America. It occurs in every Canadian province, Alaska and all of the lower 48 states.

FEEDING HABITS: Beaver forage on the bark and twigs of trees such as aspen, willow, birch, maple, alder, cherry and poplar. In summer the beaver's diet is supplemented with herbaceous vegetation such as water lilies, pondweeds and cattails. During fall, the beaver builds a food cache of branches and twigs which provides food throughout the winter when the pond ices over. In some southern areas beaver do not construct food caches but feed instead on submerged herbaceous vegetation during the winter.

BEHAVIOR: The beaver alters its environment by constructing dams and creating ponds of flowages. Beaver ponds afford protection from predators and are used to float wood for dam or lodge construction, or to the food cache. The lodge usually is built in the pond and is surrounded by water. The lodge is used by all members of the beaver family. Some beavers reside in banks of streams rather than lodges. Although chiefly nocturnal, beavers occasionally are active during the day. They live in territorial family groups called colonies composed of the two adults and their offspring (kits and yearlings). Two-year-old beavers are forced to leave the colony by the parents. More than one colony may occupy a lake or stream drainage, but territories rarely overlap. Beaver can become a nuisance by felling trees, plugging road culverts and water control structures and flooding timber and cropland. Beaver activity on certain streams can be detrimental to trout fisheries by increasing water temperatures and silt deposition and impeding fish migration. In other situations beaver are beneficial in slowing runoff waters, reducing silt losses and creating new wetland habitats for a myriad of other wildlife species.

REPRODUCTION: Beaver breed in midwinter and have a gestation period of 100 to

110 days. The single litter of 2 to 5 precocial kits are weaned at approximately 2½ months of age. Kits do little work during their first year. Adults are sexually mature at two years of age but seldom breed until their third year. Males are monogamous and females are monestrous. Kit rearing is the responsibility of the female.

POPULATION STATUS: By the turn of the 20th century beaver were a rarity, existing in only a few isolated pockets in North America. Changing land-use policies and beaver trap-transplant programs have since returned this species to most of its historic range. Beaver populations are increasing in most areas, especially western Canada and the southeastern United States, east of the Mississippi River. The beaver probably is more abundant now than it was historically.

UTILIZATION: The beaver is credited with being almost solely responsible for the rapid settlement of parts of North America. The European demand for beaver felt hats and furs for clothing was nearly insatiable. Today beaver pelts are used for making coats and accessory garments while the castoreum is used as a fixative for perfumes. Beaver primarily are taken by trapping, although shooting is permitted in some areas. Recent North American beaver harvests have yielded approximately 600,000 pelts annually. The total value of the pelts and castor glands is about 10 million dollars annually. Beaver meat is consumed by some trappers and their families, who consider it a delicacy.

REFERENCES

ANON. 1962. Beaver in Saskatchewan. Conservation Bulletin No. 1, Department of Natural Resources, Saskatoon, Sask.

_____. 1969. Beaver. Catalogue No. R69-4/2 Canadian Wildlife Service Ottawa, Ontario.

_____. 1978. Report on the Status of Canadian Wildlife Used by the Fur Industry. Department of Industry, Trade and Commerce, Ottawa, Canada.

_____. 1979. Beaver. New Brunswick Fur-Bearers No. 1. Department of Natural Resources, Fredericton, New Brunswick.

_____. 1979. Fur Production: Season 1977-78. Statistics Canada, Ottawa, Ontario. 17 pp.

BANFIELD, A.W.F. 1974. Mammals of Canada. University of Toronto Press, Toronto.

BERGERUD, A.T., and D.R. Miller. 1977. Population Dynamics of Newfoundland Beaver. Canadian Journal of Zoology. 55: 1480-1482.

BURT, W.H. 1954. The Mammals of Michigan. Univ. Mich. Press, Ann Arbor. 228 pp.

_____, and R.P. Grossenheider. 1976. A Field Guide to the Mammals. 3rd Edition. Houghton Mifflin Co., Boston. 289 pp.

DEEMS, E.F., and D. Pursley. 1978. North American Furbearers, Their Management, Research and Harvest Status in 1976. International Association of Fish and Wildlife Agencies. 171 pp.

GUNDERSON, H.L., and J.R. Beer. 1953. The Mammals of Minnesota. Univ. Minn. Press, Minneapolis. 190 pp.

HODGDON, H.E., and J.S. Larson. 1980. A Bibliography of the Recent Literature on Beaver. Research Bull. No. 665. Mass. Agr. Exp. Station. U. of Mass., Amherst. 128 pp.

NOVAK, M. 1972. Beaver in Ontario. Ministry of Natural Resources, Toronto, Ontario. 20 pp.

SLOUGH, B.G., and R.M.R.S. Saddler. 1977. A Land Capability Classification System for Beaver. Canadian Journal of Zoology. 55(8): 1324-1355.

TODD, A.W. 1978. Methodology used for Alberta Land Inventory of Furbearers. Alberta Fish & Wildlife Division, Recreation Parks and Wildlife. 66 p.

Van NOSTRAND, N.S., and A.B. Stephanson. 1964. Age Determination for Beaver by Tooth Development. Journal of Wildlife Management. 28(3): 430-434.

_____. 1977. Determining the Average Size and Composition of Beaver Families. Journal of Wildlife Management. 41(4): 751-754.

NOVAKOWSKI, N.S. 1965. Population Dynamics of a Beaver Population in Northern Latitudes. Ph.D. diss., University of Saskatchewan, Saskatoon. 154 p.

Map 2. The Range of the Beaver in the United States and Canada.

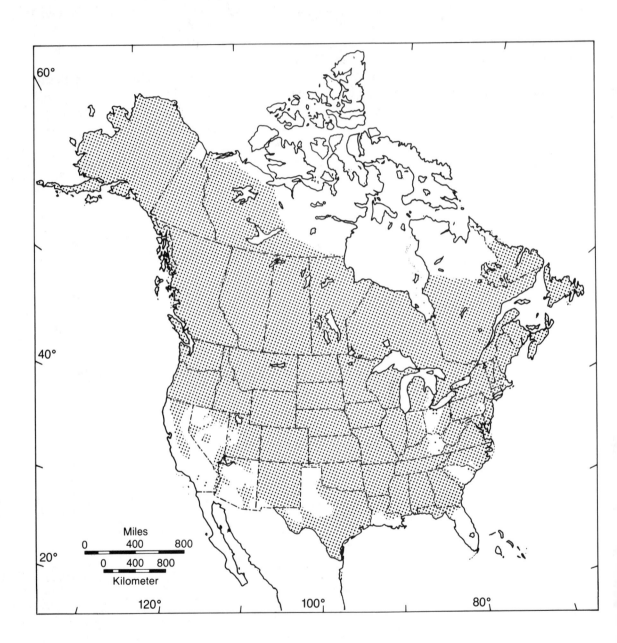

Fig. 2 — The Management Status of the Beaver in the United States and Canada

STATES, PROVINCES AND TERRITORIES	Present	Total Protection	Hunting Season	Trapping Season	Year-Round Harvesting	Limited Harvesting	Food Resource	Habitat Management	Population Inventories	Special Regulations	Private Lands Leased
United States											
Alabama	●		●	●	●		●			●	
Alaska	●			●		●	●		●		
Arizona	●			●		●		●		●	
Arkansas	●		●	●	●		●				
California	●			●		●					
Colorado	●		●	●	●			●	●	●	
Connecticut	●			●		●	●	●	●	●	
Delaware	●	●				●					
Florida	●				●					●	
Georgia	●			●	●		●	●		●	
Idaho	●			●		●			●	●	
Illinois	●			●		●	●	●	●	●	
Indiana	●			●		●	●	●			
Iowa	●			●		●	●	●	●	●	
Kansas	●			●		●	●				
Kentucky	●			●		●					
Louisiana	●			●		●					
Maine	●			●		●			●	●	
Maryland	●			●		●	●	●	●		
Massachusetts	●			●		●					
Michigan	●			●		●	●	●	●	●	
Minnesota	●			●		●	●		●	●	
Mississippi	●		●	●		●			●	●	
Missouri	●			●		●	●	●	●		
Montana	●			●		●		●	●	●	●
Nebraska	●			●		●	●			●	
Nevada	●			●		●		●			
New Hampshire	●			●		●	●	●	●	●	
New Jersey	●			●		●	●	●	●		
New Mexico	●			●		●		●	●	●	
New York	●			●		●		●	●	●	
North Carolina	●			●		●	●				●
United States (Cont'd)											
North Dakota	●		●	●		●		●	●		
Ohio	●			●			●		●	●	
Oklahoma	●		●	●		●		●			
Oregon	●			●		●				●	
Pennsylvania	●			●		●		●			
Rhode Island	●	●							●	●	
South Carolina	●			●		●		●		●	
South Dakota	●			●		●					
Tennessee	●		●	●		●					
Texas	●			●	●					●	
Utah	●			●		●			●		
Vermont	●			●		●			●	●	
Virginia	●			●		●	●	●		●	
Washington	●			●		●			●		
West Virginia	●			●		●	●	●	●	●	
Wisconsin	●			●		●	●	●	●	●	
Wyoming	●			●		●	●	●			
Total (United States)	49	2	6	46	7	39	27	17	31	28	2
Canada											
Alberta	●			●		●	●		●	●	
British Columbia	●			●		●	●				●
Manitoba	●			●		●	●		●	●	
New Brunswick	●			●			●	●	●		
Newfoundland	●			●		●			●	●	
Northwest Territories	●			●			●				
Nova Scotia	●			●		●	●		●	●	
Ontario	●			●		●	●		●		
Prince Edward Island	●			●		●	●		●	●	
Quebec	●			●		●	●		●		●
Saskatchewan	●			●		●	●		●	●	
Yukon Territory	●			●		●	●		●		
Total (Canada)	12	0	0	12	0	10	11	1	10	7	2

45

MUSKRAT
(*Ondatra zibethicus*)

DESCRIPTION: The muskrat is medium sized, round-bodied rodent with small ears and short legs. The tail is long, black, nearly naked and flattened laterally. An edging of short stiff hairs is visible along the underside of the tail and along the margins of the large webbed hind feet. The front feet are webless and much smaller than the hind feet. The pelage varies from dark brown to black and the belly fur is lighter in color than the guard hairs and underfur on the head and back. Sexes are alike in appearance. Adults attain lengths of 10 to 14 inches (25-35 cm) excluding the 8 to 11 inch (20-28 cm) tail. They generally weigh 2 to 4 pounds (0.9-1.8 kg) when full grown. The skull has 16 teeth. There are 6 mammae.

HABITAT: Muskrats inhabit fresh and saltwater wetlands and waterways in every North American province and state except Florida.

FEEDING HABITS: Muskrats primarily are herbivorous. They prefer aquatic plants — roots, bulbs and foliage of cattails, pondweeds, rushes, sedges and wild rice. They also eat tree roots and agricultural crops. Green algae is an important food in large, deep bodies of water where emergent plant growth is not abundant. When herbaceous foods diminish muskrats will eat fish, amphibians, reptiles, mussels and insects. High populations of muskrats have caused extensive damages ("eat-outs") in some wetlands. An eat-out describes a situation in a pond or marsh where muskrats have severely depleted the existing aquatic vegetation including the root systems which bind the organic soils together. This converts the pond or marsh to a mucky area and destroys waterfowl, fish and other wetland wildlife habitat.

BEHAVIOR: Muskrats are nocturnal and crepuscular and seldom are seen outside of their lodges and burrows in daytime. They are chiefly aquatic, however in the fall and under freeze-out conditions muskrats often travel considerable distances overland. During this time they appear to be more aggressive and are more vulnerable to predators. Muskrats dig tunnels (commonly called burrows or "leads") and build conical structures (nesting lodges, feeding houses and push ups or "breathers") using vegetative materials, sticks and mud. Both tunnels and vegetative structures provide protection during feeding, resting, mating and parturition. The muskrat's burrowing and feeding activities can be detrimental to fields, roads, pond fills and agricultural crops.

REPRODUCTION: The muskrat, like most rodents, is a very prolific animal. Females are fertile in varying estrous cycles during the year dependent upon latitude. The males' sexual condition apparently controls the timing and extent of breeding activities. In the North muskrats generally breed between April and September while in the South breeding occurs throughout the year. Muskrats are promiscuous and pair bonding does not occur. The gestation period is 28 to 30 days and females give birth to 1 to 5 litters each year. Litters average 5 to 6 altricial young that are dependent on their mother for approximately one month. Muskrats become sexually mature at 6 or 7 months of age in the south and females born in the early spring can mate in the fall of the same year.

POPULATION STATUS: Muskrat populations, historically, were and still are abundant and relatively stable in North America. Major short term fluctuations are primarily in response to habitat conditions. Their wide distribution and great abundance underline the paramount importance of muskrats in North America's wild fur industry.

UTILIZATION: Muskrat pelts are extremely versatile and relatively durable. They are used in both "long" and "short" fur styles and in full length garments and trim. Pelts with guard hairs intact render a "long-fur" appearance while pelts with guard hairs removed resemble the pelt of a fur seal. Such pelts are called "Hudson Seal" among fur traders. In recent years the annual North American muskrat harvest has varied between 7 and 10 million pelts for total annual market values of 35 to 45 million dollars. Muskrat meat is considered to be a delicacy and hundreds of thousands of muskrat carcasses are sold for human consumption each year.

REFERENCES

ANONYMOUS. 1978. Report of the Status of Canadian Wildlife used by the Fur Industry. Revised Edition (1977). Department of Industry, Trade and Commerce, Ottawa, Canada, in Association with the Canada Fur Council.

ANTHONY, H.E. 1928. Field Book of North American Mammals. G. P. Putnam's Sons, New York. 674 pp.

BANFIELD, A.W.F. 1974. The Mammals of Canada. Univ. of Toronto Press. 438 pp.

BESHEARS, W.W. and A.O. Haugen. 1953. Muskrats in Relation to Farm Ponds. Jour. Wild. Management. 17: 451-455.

BURT, W.H., and R.P. Grossenheider. 1964. A Field Guide to the Mammals. Houghton Mifflin Co., Boston. 289 pp.

DORNEY, R.S., and A.J. Rusch. 1953. Muskrat Growth and Litter Production. Tech. Wildl. Bull. 8, Wisc. Cons. Dept., Madison, Wisc. 32 pp.

DOZIER, H.L. 1948. Estimating Muskrat Populations by House Counts. Wild. Leaflet 306, Wash., D.C. 17 pp.

ERRINGTON, P.L. 1978. Muskrats and Marsh Management. Univ. Neb. Press, Lincoln, Neb. 183 pp.

GASHWILER, J.S. 1948. Maine Muskrat Investigations. Maine Dept. of Fish and Game, Augusta, Maine. 38 pp.

HALL, E.R., and K.R. Kelson. 1959. Mammals of North America. Ronald Press Co., New York. 1083 pp.

MATHIAK, H.A. 1966. Muskrat Populations Studies at Horican Marsh. Tech. Bull. 36, Wisc. Cons. Dept., Madison, Wisc. 56 pp.

_____ and A. F. Linde. 1954. Role of Refuges in Muskrat Management. Tech. Wild. Bull. 10, Wisc. Cons. Dept., Madison, Wisc. 25 pp.

McLEOD, J.A., and G.F. Bondar. 1952. Studies on the Biology of the Muskrat in Manitoba. Canadian J. of Zool. 30: 243-253.

O'NEIL, T. 1949. The Muskrat in Louisiana Marshes. La. Dept. Wildl. and Fish. 152 pp.

PETERSON, Randolph L. 1966. The Mammals of Eastern Canada. Toronto, Oxford University Press.

WALKER, E.P. 1975. Mammals of the World (third ed.). Johns Hopkins Press, Baltimore, Maryland. 1500 pp.

WILLNER, G.R., J.A. Chapman and J.R. Goldsberry. 1975. A Study and Review of Muskrat Food Habits with Special Reference to Maryland. Waverly Press Inc. 24 pp.

Map 3. The Range of the Muskrat in the United States and Canada.

Fig. 3   The Management Status of the Muskrat in the United States and Canada

STATES, PROVINCES AND TERRITORIES	Present	Total Protection	Hunting Season	Trapping Season	Year-Round Harvesting	Limited Harvesting	Food Resource	Habitat Management	Population Inventories	Special Regulations	Private Lands Leased
United States											
Alabama	●			●		●	●			●	
Alaska	●			●		●	●	●			
Arizona	●		●	●		●				●	
Arkansas	●		●	●		●					
California	●			●		●					
Colorado	●		●	●		●					
Connecticut	●			●		●	●	●		●	
Delaware	●			●			●				●
Florida											
Georgia	●			●		●	●			●	
Idaho	●			●		●					
Illinois	●			●		●	●		●	●	
Indiana	●			●		●	●	●	●		
Iowa	●			●		●	●	●	●	●	
Kansas	●			●		●					
Kentucky	●			●		●					
Louisiana	●			●		●		●	●	●	●
Maine	●			●		●					
Maryland	●			●		●	●	●		●	●
Massachusetts	●			●		●					
Michigan	●			●		●	●		●		
Minnesota	●			●		●	●	●		●	
Mississippi	●			●		●	●			●	
Missouri	●			●		●	●	●	●	●	
Montana	●			●		●				●	●
Nebraska	●			●		●	●			●	
Nevada	●			●		●			●		
New Hampshire	●			●		●			●	●	●
New Jersey	●			●		●	●	●	●		●
New Mexico	●			●							
New York	●			●		●	●		●	●	●
North Carolina	●			●		●	●				●
United States (Cont'd)											
North Dakota	●			●		●			●		●
Ohio	●			●		●	●	●	●		
Oklahoma	●		●	●		●					
Oregon	●			●		●					●
Pennsylvania	●			●		●					
Rhode Island	●			●		●			●	●	
South Carolina	●		●	●		●				●	
South Dakota	●			●		●					
Tennessee	●		●	●		●		●			●
Texas	●		●	●	●					●	●
Utah	●			●	●			●	●	●	
Vermont	●		●	●		●					
Virginia	●			●				●			●
Washington	●			●		●			●		
West Virginia	●			●		●	●				
Wisconsin	●			●		●	●	●		●	●
Wyoming	●			●		●					
Total (United States)	48	0	8	48	2	43	21	13	16	20	13
Canada											
Alberta	●			●		●	●		●	●	
British Columbia	●			●		●	●				●
Manitoba	●			●		●	●	●	●	●	●
New Brunswick	●			●					●	●	
Newfoundland	●			●		●	●				
Northwest Territories	●			●		●	●				
Nova Scotia	●			●			●				
Ontario	●			●					●		
Prince Edward Island	●			●		●	●	●		●	●
Quebec	●			●		●	●		●		
Saskatchewan	●			●		●	●			●	
Yukon Territory	●			●		●	●			●	
Total (Canada)	12	0	0	12	0	10	10	3	5	5	3

50

NUTRIA
(*Myocaster coypus*)

DESCRIPTION: The nutria is similar in appearance to a beaver except for its round hairless tail and less massive head. The guard hair is light brown to blackish brown and somewhat shaggy in appearance. The underfur is grayish in color. Nutria have thick bodies and short legs. The front feet are relatively small and webless while the hind feet are large and webbed. Sexes are alike except males are larger than females. Adult males average 15 pounds (6.8 kg) in weight and 40 inches (101 cm) in total length while adult females average 13 pounds (5.9 kg) in weight and 38 inches (96 cm) in length. The skull has 20 teeth and the four large incisors are reddish-orange in color. There are 8 to 10 mammae which are located dorso-laterally. The mammae are above the waterline when the animal is swimming or floating. This permits the young to nurse while the female is floating in water or in an upright position on land.

HABITAT: The nutria is most abundant in coastal marshes and swamps but it also inhabits rivers, lakes, streams, backwater areas and drainage ditches.

FEEDING HABITS: Nutria are strictly herbivorous. Their diet includes a wide variety of plants such as alligator weed, hydrocotyle, eleocharis, maiden cane, bagscale, three-square rush, hog cane, duckweed, water hyacinth, cattail and agricultural crops. Depredating nutria have caused damage in rice, sugar cane and cornfields. Nutria tend to prefer stem and leaf materials during the warmer months, and roots and rhizomes during the winter months.

BEHAVIOR: Nutria move adeptly on land, however they are agile swimmers and much more "at home" in the water. They tend to be nocturnal although they are frequently active in the daytime. Nutria feed both on land and in water. On land they construct vegetation "platforms" which are used for feeding, grooming and resting. Unlike muskrats and beaver, nutria do not build houses, lodges or extensive burrows. In some areas they dig relatively shallow burrows or shelter cavities with entrances above the water level. Nutria vocalizations are similar to the sound of a human baby crying.

REPRODUCTION: Nutria are promiscuous and breed year round. Severe winter weather, especially in the northern portion of the nutria's range, decreases or interrupts reproduction. Ovulation rates decrease, embryo resorption and abortion increase, therefore litters are smaller and/or absent in extensive periods of severe winter weather. The northern limits of the nutria's range in North America appear to be directly related to the severity of winter weather conditions. The gestation period is approximately 130 days and litter sizes range from 1 to 9 (average is 4). The precocious young are weaned at 5 to 7 weeks of age. Males attain sexual maturity at about 6 months of age while females reach sexual maturity prior to 6 months of age.

POPULATION STATUS: The nutria, originally introduced into the U.S. and Canada from South America, now is established in 15 states. It also was widely introduced into western Europe. Most U.S. introductions of nutria were escapees from fur ranches, but many releases into the wild were intentional. In Louisiana, some nutria releases were made for the purpose of controlling undesirable marsh vegetation. Nutria are considered to be valuable furbearers in some regions but in other areas they are unwanted pests. In

Louisiana, nutria originally were classified as outlaw quadrupeds but now they account for over 60 percent of the state's annual fur harvest. Many researches and wildlife managers maintain that nutria have detrimental affects on muskrat populations and their habitat.

UTILIZATION: The word nutria is a modification of the Spanish word lutra. The name lutra has been applied to various aquatic mammals including the present species and the river otter. Nutria is the common name used widely in America literature. Nutria is a versatile fur. It is used in plucked, clipped, sheared and natural forms. Pelts often are dyed shades of black, brown, beige and pastels. Plucked and sheared furs are traditionally used for luxury garments. Unplucked, natural skins are used for more casual wear — coats, jackets, parkas and for linings and trimmings. In recent years the U.S. annual harvest of nutria has been about 2 million pelts (mostly from Louisiana), valued at nearly 11 million dollars. Nutria meat, considered to be a delicacy, is widely used for human consumption in some regions of the world.

REFERENCES

BURT, W.H., and R.P. Grossenheider. 1964. A Field Guide to the Mammals. Houghton Mifflin Co., Boston. 289 pp.

DEEMS, E.F., and D. Pursley. 1978. North American Furbearers, Their Management, Research and Harvest Status in 1976. International Association of Fish and Wildlife Agencies. 171 pp.

LOWERY, G.H. 1974. The Mammals of Louisiana and its Adjacent Waters. The Louisiana State Univ. Press, Baton Rouge. 565 pp.

O'NEIL, T., and G. Linscombe. 1979. The Fur Animals, the Alligator, and the Fur Industry in Louisiana. La. Dept. of Wildl. and Fisheries Ed. Bull. 106., New Orleans. 66 pp.

SHIRLEY, M. G. 1979. Foods of Nutria in Fresh Marshes of Southeastern Louisiana. M.S. Thesis, Louisiana State University.

WILLNER, G.R., J.A. Chapman and D. Pursley. 1979. Reproduction, Physiological Responses, Food Habits, and Abundance of Nutria on Maryland Marshes. Wildlife Monographs. April. No. 65.

Map 4.   The Range of the Nutria in the United States and Canada.

Fig. 4

The Management Status of the Nutria in the United States and Canada

STATES, PROVINCES AND TERRITORIES	Present	Total Protection	Hunting Season	Trapping Season	Year-Round Harvesting	Limited Harvesting	Food Resource	Habitat Management	Population Inventories	Special Regulations	Private Lands Leased
United States											
Alabama	•		•	•	•		•			•	
Alaska											
Arizona											
Arkansas	•		•	•	•						
California											
Colorado											
Connecticut											
Delaware	•						•				
Florida	•						•			•	
Georgia	•			•		•				•	
Idaho	•		•	•	•						
Illinois											
Indiana											
Iowa											
Kansas											
Kentucky											
Louisiana	•		•	•		•	•	•		•	•
Maine											
Maryland	•		•	•	•		•			•	•
Massachusetts											
Michigan											
Minnesota											
Mississippi											
Missouri	•			•	•						
Montana											
Nebraska											
Nevada											
New Hampshire											
New Jersey											
New Mexico	•			•	•						
New York											
North Carolina	•			•	•		•				
United States (Cont'd)											
North Dakota											
Ohio											
Oklahoma											
Oregon	•			•	•						
Pennsylvania											
Rhode Island											
South Carolina											
South Dakota											
Tennessee											
Texas	•						•		•	•	•
Utah											
Vermont											
Virginia	•		•	•	•		•			•	
Washington	•				•				•		
West Virginia											
Wisconsin											
Wyoming											
Total (United States)	15	0	6	11	12	3	6	1	1	7	3
Canada											
Alberta											
British Columbia											
Manitoba											
New Brunswick											
Newfoundland											
Northwest Territories											
Nova Scotia											
Ontario	•										
Prince Edward Island											
Quebec											
Saskatchewan											
Yukon Territory											
Total (Canada)	1	0	0	0	0	0	0	0	0	0	0

SECTION III
ORDER CARNIVORA

COYOTE
(Canis latrans)

DESCRIPTION: Coyotes are similar in appearance to medium-sized dogs. They have long, slender muzzles, relatively large pointed ears, long slender legs, relatively small feet and a bushy tail that is less than half the total body length. The tail usually is carried below the level of the back or even between the hind legs when the coyote is running as compared to the wolf, which usually carries its tail high. Pelage color ranges from black-tipped off-white to rusty brown but usually is a buff grizzled-gray. The muzzle, backs of ears and forelegs usually are a rusty color, while the throat and belly are white or gray. Male coyotes are larger than females. Adults range from 41 to 53 inches (105-135 cm) in length and weigh from 20 to 50 pounds (9-22 kg). The skull has 42 teeth. There are 8 mammae.

HABITAT: Coyotes are extremely adaptable. They generally are associated with open areas but apparently prefer hilly terrain with bluffs and brushy areas. The coyote is one of the few wild animals that has adjusted to man-disturbed environments and thrives in close proximity to man.

FEEDING HABITS: Coyotes are opportunistic scavengers. Although rodents and rabbits comprise the bulk of their diets, coyotes readily eat carrion and plant foods. In some areas the opportunity to prey on domestic livestock as permitted by man allows the coyote's feeding habits to cause problems. The greatest problem is sheep depredation, but coyotes are also known to prey sometimes on calves, pigs, poultry and even ripening watermelons. Coyotes apparently are losing their fear of humans in some suburban areas.

BEHAVIOR: Often regarded as nocturnal and shy, coyotes sometimes exhibit diurnal activity patterns. When in close association with man in undisturbed (no trapping or hunting) situations coyotes are becoming less timid and are frequently seen during daylight hours. Coyotes hunt singly or at times in aggregations of as many as a dozen individuals. The basic "social unit", however, consists only of the family group. These units sometimes form relays during hunting operations. Coyotes are the fleetest of North American canids, reaching speeds of up to 40 miles (65 km) per hour for short distances. In addition to the chase-method of hunting, coyotes employ the stiff-legged "mousing" technique, characteristic of foxes when hunting small mammals. An apparently unique hunting relationship sometimes exists between coyotes and badgers, whereby coyotes will follow a hunting badger and capture those prey species missed by the digging badger.

REPRODUCTION: Coyotes probably pair for life, or until one member of the pair dies. Adult females are monestrous, in heat, for 4 to 5 days between late January and late March. Adult males are sexually active throughout the late winter - early spring period. The number of young females that breed each year is affected by the local coyote population's density and food availability. Proportionately more young-of-the-year coyote females breed in situations of low coyote densities and high food abundance. The female coyote is solely responsible for den preparation and maintenance. Gestation is about 63 days and the pups are born from early April to mid May. Litters contain from one to more than 12 pups, although the average is five to six. The altricial pups are blind and helpless at birth and are covered with brownish-gray wooly fur. Their eyes open at 8 to

14 days of age. The male coyote assists in raising the young and initially he supplies most of the food for the female and newborn pups. At weaning time, about eight weeks of age, both parents carry food in their stomachs to the den and then regurgitate it for the pups. In contrast to a fox den, the periphery of a coyote's den usually is clean, with no large collection of bones or other carrion. The pups are taught to hunt when they are 8 to 12 weeks old and the family group usually breaks up in the fall as the young disperse. Although several members of a coyote family may still be hunting together in midwinter, coyotes do not form true packs as do wolves. During the period of November through March, young coyotes disperse into new areas. The average distance traveled is from 10 to 25 miles (16-40 km) but may be as far as 100 miles (161 km).

POPULATION STATUS: Prior to 1900, the coyote's range was restricted to areas west of the Mississippi in the United States and west of Ontario's Lake Nipigon in Canada. Since that time coyotes have expanded their range eastward into the east coast mainland provinces of Canada, some southeastern states and New England in the United States. The coyote's ability to breed with other similar canids, especially domestic or feral dogs, has caused problems with taxonomic identification and nomenclature in eastern North America. Under favorable conditons, coyote populations obtain densities of 5 to 6 animals per square mile (2.6 km²) but average densities usually are about one coyote per square mile. Adult male coyotes usually establish home ranges of 10 to 20 square miles (26-52 km²) while mature females range over smaller areas. Coyote numbers appear to be increasing in many areas despite heavy utilization by man. In some areas coyote numbers appear to fluctuate in response to cyclical prey populations. The late summer population of coyotes in North America probably exceeds two million animals. In some areas where coyotes are classified as furbearers, regulated harvests often cannot keep pace with the coyote's reproduction rate. In such areas control measures frequently are required to keep the coyote population within acceptable agricultural depredation levels.

UTILIZATION: Coyotes are hunted and trapped for their pelts. In addition to trapping techniques, hunting methods include the use of trailing and sight hounds, and predator calls. Recent North American coyote harvests have yielded nearly 600,000 pelts valued at more than 30 million dollars annually.

REFERENCES

ANONYMOUS. Report of the Status of Canadian Wildlife Used by the Fur Industry. Revised Edition (1977). Department of Industry, Trade & Commerce, Ottawa, Canada, in Association with the Canada Fur Council.

_____. 1978. Predator Damage in the West: a Study of Coyote Management Alternatives. U.S. Fish and Wildlife Service. Dept. of Interior, Washington, D.C. 168 pp.

BANFIELD, A.W.F. 1974. The Mammals of Canada. Univ. Toronto Press. 438 pp.

BURT, W.H., and R.P. Grossenheider. 1964. A Field Guide to the Mammals. Houghton Mifflin Company, Boston. 289 pp.

DEEMS, E.F., and D. Pursley. 1978. North American Furbearers, Their Management, Research and Harvest Status in 1976. International Association of Fish and Wildlife Agencies. 171 pp.

GEE, C.K., and R. Magleby. 1976. Characteristics of Sheep Production in the Western United States. Agric. Econ. Rept. 345, U.S. Dept. Agric., Econ. Res. Serv., Wash.,

D.C. 47 pp.

GIER, H.T. 1957. Coyotes in Kansas. Kansas State Univ., Manhattan, Kansas. Bulletin 393, 95 pp.

HALL, E.R., and K.R. Kelson. 1959. The Mammals of North America. Vols. 1, 2. The Ronald Press Company, New York. 1083 pp.

HENDERSON, F.R., E.K. Boggess, and B. A. Brown. 1977b. Understanding the Coyote. Coop. Ext. Serv., Kansas State Univ., Manhattan. No. C578. 23 pp.

_____. 1980. Coyotes as an Aesthetic and Renewable Resource. Symposium Proceedings Utah State University, Logan Utah. April 23-24.

KNOWLTON, F.F. 1972. Preliminary Interpretations of Coyote Population Mechanics with some Management Implications. J. Wildl. Manage. 36(2): 369-382.

PETERSON, Randolph L. 1966. The Mammals of Eastern Canada. Toronto, Oxford University Press.

WALKER, E.P. 1975. Mammals of the World (third ed.). Johns Hopkins Press, Baltimore, Maryland. 1500 pp.

YOUNG, S.P., and H.H.T. Jackson. 1951. The Clever Coyote. The Stackpole Co., Harrisburg, Pa. 411 pp.

Map 5. **The Range of the Coyote in the United States and Canada.**

Fig. 5

The Management Status of the Coyote in the United States and Canada

STATES, PROVINCES AND TERRITORIES	Present	Total Protection	Hunting Season	Trapping Season	Year-Round Harvesting	Limited Harvesting	Food Resource	Habitat Management	Population Inventories	Special Regulations	Private Lands Leased
United States											
Alabama	●		●	●	●						
Alaska	●		●	●		●					
Arizona	●		●	●		●		●		●	
Arkansas	●		●	●	●						
California	●		●	●	●				●		
Colorado	●		●	●	●						
Connecticut	●		●	●		●					
Delaware											
Florida	●					●				●	
Georgia	●					●					
Idaho	●		●	●	●						
Illinois	●		●	●		●			●	●	
Indiana	●		●	●		●			●		
Iowa	●		●	●	●				●	●	
Kansas	●		●	●	●				●	●	
Kentucky	●		●	●	●				●		
Louisiana	●		●	●	●						
Maine	●			●		●			●	●	
Maryland											
Massachusetts	●	●									
Michigan	●				●						
Minnesota	●				●				●	●	
Mississippi	●				●						
Missouri	●		●	●	●	●			●	●	
Montana	●				●				●		
Nebraska	●				●						
Nevada	●				●						
New Hampshire	●				●				●	●	
New Jersey	●	●									
New Mexico	●				●						
New York	●		●	●	●						
North Carolina	●	●									
United States (Cont'd)											
North Dakota	●		●	●	●				●	●	
Ohio	●										
Oklahoma	●		●	●	●					●	
Oregon	●			●	●				●		
Pennsylvania	●			●	●						
Rhode Island	●	●							●	●	
South Carolina											
South Dakota	●		●	●	●				●		
Tennessee	●		●	●		●					
Texas	●				●						
Utah	●				●						
Vermont	●		●	●	●						
Virginia	●				●						
Washington	●				●				●		
West Virginia	●				●						
Wisconsin	●		●	●	●						
Wyoming	●		●	●	●						
Total (United States)	46	4	23	26	32	10	0	1	16	12	0
Canada											
Alberta	●		●	●		●			●	●	
British Columbia	●		●	●	●						
Manitoba	●			●		●				●	
New Brunswick	●		●	●					●		
Newfoundland											
Northwest Territories	●		●		●						
Nova Scotia	●		●	●							
Ontario	●		●	●	●				●		
Prince Edward Island											
Quebec	●		●	●	●						
Saskatchewan	●			●						●	
Yukon Territory	●		●	●		●				●	
Total (Canada)	10	0	8	9	4	3	0	0	3	4	0

GRAY WOLF
(*Canis lupus*)

DESCRIPTION: The gray wolf, the largest North American canid, is similar in appearance to a large German shepherd dog. It is deep-chested with long legs and proportionately large feet. The tail is relatively short and, unlike the coyote's, is held high when running. The skull is massive with a broader muzzle and more distinct brow line than other North American canids. The nose pad is generally greater than one inch (2.5 cm) in width. The pelage color varies from white (in the far north) to black, although most wolf skins are a mixture of gray, brown and black with light underparts like the coyote. In early winter immature wolves exhibit more uniform coloration and woolier coats than adults. The gray wolf's ears are proportionately smaller and more rounded than the coyote's. The sexes are alike in appearance except males are larger than females. Some males exceed 6 feet (1.8 m) in total length and stand nearly 3 feet (0.9 m) high at the shoulders. Adult gray wolves range from 59 to 81 inches (149-205 cm) in total length including the 14 to 20 inch (36-50 cm) tail and weigh from 57 to 175 pounds (26-79 kg). Alaskan wolves generally weigh 80 to 120 pounds (36-54 kg) while wolves south of Canada usually weigh only 60 to 100 pounds (27-45 kg). The skull has 42 teeth. There are 8 mammae.

HABITAT: The gray wolf utilizes a wide range of habitats from the high arctic polar desert of the Arctic Archipelago to the aspen parkland and agricultural zones of southern Canada. Wolves originally inhabited all North American habitats that contained their ungulate prey species. In early times the gray wolf was largely replaced by the red wolf (*Canis niger*) in a crescent of range extending from east Texas to Florida and north to southern Missouri. Gray wolves tend to prefer successional forests that favor deer or moose production. Historically, the central grasslands were prime wolf habitat when hordes of bison roamed the plains.

FEEDING HABITS: The gray wolf is characteristically a predator of "big game" animals. In early America the wolf's primary prey species were deer, elk, moose, caribou, mountain sheep, bison and pronghorns. The beaver was the only other significant species in the wolf's diet. Apparently, a wolf population cannot sustain itself on small mammals alone although in northern areas wolves can temporarily utilize snowshoe hares as sole food sources when hares are abundant. Occasionally, gray wolves kill and sometimes eat other carnivores such as coyotes, foxes and bobcats as well as raccoons, muskrats and other small mammals. In summer wolf pups often eat mice and lemmings and occasionally fruits such as blueberries, although wolves usually are strictly carnivorous. Wolves readily feed on carrion at anytime of the year.

BEHAVIOR: The most striking behavioral characteristic which distinguishes wolves from other wild North American canids is the highly structured social unit usually comprised of related individuals. The social behavior extends through all facets of pack activities from hierarchial reproductive regulatory mechanisms, to hunting techniques and even to vocalizations of pack members. The social unit consists of a family group composed of parents, pups and close relatives. Social hierarchy follows a pattern where the largest and strongest male is the leader, followed by senile or younger males, then the mate of the leader, other females and lastly the pups in order of strength. The average pack contains 4 to 7 wolves but pack sizes vary from 2 to 14 members. Although larger packs have been recorded, they usually represent short-term and unstable aggregations of wolves immediately following a highly successful breeding season. Lone wolves and non-breeding groups of 2 to 4 animals are common. All members take part in pack maintenance from procuring food to "babysitting" the pups. There is much socializing amongst the members. Strange wolves usually are not accepted by the pack and may be attacked and killed by pack members although several packs may unite during the winter for hunting. A wolf pack utilizes around the den a home range, which may be 100 to 300 square miles (259-777 km²) in size. Wolf territories are marked by urination posts which establish the boundaries. Seasonal wolf migrations sometimes occur in Alaska, and in northern Canada these movements may be as great as 500 miles (805 km) when following migrating caribou herds. Often dependent upon prey density, wolf densities range from one wolf per 10 square miles (26 km²) to one wolf per 80 square miles (207 km²). Wolves are not particularly fast but may attain a speed of 28 miles (45 km) per hour for short distances. Most big game species can run faster than wolves, except in deep snow, swamps or on smooth ice, so wolves resort to a hunting strategy which gives them a decided advantage over their prey. The wolf pack will outflank the prey, form chase relays or sometimes part of the pack may drive the quarry towards the other waiting pack members. Gray wolves are primarily nocturnal but frequently are active in the daytime.

REPRODUCTION: Wolves apparently mate for life and within the normal social structure of the pack usually only the dominant pair breed. Following a disruption of the social hierarchy (usually man-induced) all females within the pack may breed causing a local population explosion. The females are monestrous and are in heat for a five day period in late winter, usually late February to mid-March. Litters contain from 5 to 14 pups (7 is average). Parturition usually occurs in early May after a gestation period of 30 to 60 days. The pups are sooty-gray in color, blind, and pug-nosed with floppy ears. Their eyes open and ears become erect at 5 to 9 days of age. The first adult coat replaces the wooly puppy coat at about one month of age. Between 6 to 8 weeks of age the pups are weaned. Weaning is a gradual process because the pups are dependent upon regurgitated meat from adult pack members. When the pups are about 2 months old the female moves them to a summer den or an open-air "rendezvous site" near water which becomes the pack's headquarters until another move is necessary. The pups accompany the adults on hunting forays by late August or early September. Care of the young is shared by both parents as well as by other members of the pack. Females become sexually mature at two years of age but males do not reach sexual maturity until they are three years old.

POPULATION STATUS: Over the major portion of their range, gray wolf populations are relatively stable. In the fringe areas, however, wolf numbers can fluctuate dramatically in response to human activitiy. Intensive control measures can denude small areas of wolves for short periods of time whereas minor harvesting efforts may check the population growth or occasionally cause local population explosions by removing the hierarchial control of breeding. Canada's wolf population is estimated to be 28,000 to 33,000 individuals. In most of the Canadian range, wolf populations are not jeopardized by current harvesting efforts or control measures. In the conterminous U.S. viable gray wolf populations exist only in northeastern Minnesota and on Michigan's Isle Royale, although wolves occasionally occur in northern Wisconsin and on the upper peninsula of

Michigan. However, in recent years individual wolves and tracks have been recorded in the region between Glacier and Yellowstone National Parks. These may be remnants of the Northern Rocky Mountain wolf. Occasionally wolves from Canada cross the border into Montana, Idaho and Washington, and apparently stragglers wander north across the border into the U.S. from the small population in Mexico. Since Alaska gained statehood (1959) it has given its gray wolves more legal protection than existed ever before and today wolves are numerous throughout Alaska, including the Kenai Peninsula where poison campaigns had previously extirpated them for nearly 65 years.

UTILIZATION: Gray wolves are both hunted and trapped in Alaska and all Canadian provinces except New Brunswick, Nova Scotia and Prince Edward Island. Approximately 6,000 Canadian wolf pelts are marketed annually for a total value of about $500,000 each year. And approximately 1,000 Alaskan wolf pelts are marketed for a total value of nearly $250,000 each year. Wolf pelts are used in full garments, for trimmings and accessories. The potential harvest of gray wolf pelts is estimated to be about 10,000 annually without causing a decline in the Alaska-Canada wolf population.

REFERENCES

ALLEN, D.L. 1979. Wolves of Minong. Houghton Mifflin Co., Boston. 499 pp.

ANONYMOUS. 1978. Report of the Status of Canadian Wildlife used by the Fur Industry. Revised Edition (1977). Department of Industry, Trade & Commerce, Ottawa, Canada, in Association with the Canada Fur Council.

BANFIELD, A. W. F. 1974. The Mammals of Canada. Univ. of Toronto Press. 438 pp.

BURT, W. H., and R. P. Grossenheider. 1976. A Field Guide to the Mammals. 3rd Edition. Houghton Mifflin Co., Boston. 289 pp.

HALL, E. R., and K. R. Kelson. 1959. Mammals of North America. Ronald Press Co., New York. 1083 pp.

KLINGHAMMER, E. (Ed.). 1979. The Behavior and Ecology of Wolves. Anim. Behavior Soc., Symp. Behavior and Ecology of Wolves, Prox. 588 pp.

LOPEZ, B. H. 1944. Of Wolves and Men. Chas. Scribner's Sons, N.Y. 309 pp.

MECH, L. D. 1966. The Wolves of Isle Royale. USDI, Nat. Park Service, Fauna Series 7. 210 pp.

_____. 1970. The Wolf: the Ecology and Behavior of an Endangered Species. Nat. Hist. Press, Garden City, N.Y. 384 pp.

PETERSON, R. O. 1977. Wolf Ecology and Prey Relationships on Isle Royale. USDI, Sci. Mon. Series 11. 210 pp.

PETERSON, Randolph L. 1966. The Mammals of Eastern Canada. Toronto, Oxford University Press.

RUTTER, R. J., and D. H. Pimlott. 1968. The World of the Wolf. J. B. Lippincott Co., N.Y. 202 pp.

WALKER, W. P. 1975. Mammals of the World (third ed.). Johns Hopkins Press, Baltimore, Maryland. 1500 pp.

YOUNG, S. P. 1946. The Wolf in North American History. Caxton Printers, Caldwell, Idaho. 149 pp.

_____, and E. A. Goldman. 1944. The Wolves of North America. Amer. Wildl. Inst. 636 pp.

ZIMEN, E. 1971. Wolfe and Konigspudel. R. Piper and Co., Munchen. 257 pp.

Map 6.   **The Range of the Gray Wolf in the United States and Canada.**

Miles
0   400   800

0   400   800
Kilometer

60°

40°

20°

120°   100°   80°

Fig. 6

The Management Status of the Gray Wolf in the United States and Canada

STATES, PROVINCES AND TERRITORIES	Present	Total Protection	Hunting Season	Trapping Season	Year-Round Harvesting	Limited Harvesting	Food Resource	Habitat Management	Population Inventories	Special Regulations	Private Lands Leased
United States											
Alabama											
Alaska	●		●	●		●			●		
Arizona											
Arkansas											
California											
Colorado											
Connecticut											
Delaware											
Florida											
Georgia											
Idaho	●	●							●		
Illinois											
Indiana											
Iowa											
Kansas											
Kentucky											
Louisiana											
Maine											
Maryland											
Massachusetts											
Michigan	●	●									
Minnesota	●	●							●		
Mississippi											
Missouri											
Montana	●	●									
Nebraska											
Nevada											
New Hampshire											
New Jersey											
New Mexico	●	●									
New York											
North Carolina											
United States (Cont'd)											
North Dakota		●									
Ohio											
Oklahoma											
Oregon											
Pennsylvania											
Rhode Island											
South Carolina											
South Dakota											
Tennessee											
Texas											
Utah											
Vermont											
Virginia											
Washington	●	●									
West Virginia											
Wisconsin	●	●									
Wyoming											
Total (United States)	8	8	1	1	0	1	0	0	3	0	0
Canada											
Alberta	●		●	●	●					●	
British Columbia	●		●	●	●						●
Manitoba	●		●	●		●			●	●	
New Brunswick											
Newfoundland	●			●		●					
Northwest Territories	●		●		●						
Nova Scotia											
Ontario	●		●	●	●				●		
Prince Edward Island											
Quebec	●		●	●	●						
Saskatchewan	●			●							
Yukon Territory	●		●	●						●	
Total (Canada)	9	0	7	8	5	2	0	0	2	3	1

ARCTIC FOX
(*Alopex lagopus*)

DESCRIPTION: The arctic fox is distinguished by its heavy white winter coat, compact body, small rounded ears, short snout and heavily furred feet. There are two distinct color phases, blue and white, although the summer coat of each is similar. The blue color phase is dominant on the Pribilof Islands (85%-95% are blues). The summer pelage is thinner and brown-toned. The long bushy tail accounts for about ⅓ of the total body length. Adults are 29 to 32 inches (74-84 cm) long and weigh from 6 to nearly 15 pounds (3-7 kg). Males are slightly larger than females. The skull has 42 teeth. There are 14 mammae.

HABITAT: The arctic fox inhabits the alpine and arctic tundral zones north of the timberline. It also ventures far out on the sea ice.

FEEDING HABITS: The primary food source is lemmings, but carrion also is of major importance. In the summer arctic foxes feed on ground squirrels, young birds, eggs and berries.

BEHAVIOR: The arctic fox is generally nocturnal; however, it is active during the midnight-sun-period in the summer months. It tends to be solitary except during the pup-rearing period. Arctic foxes follow polar bears onto the sea ice in search of food, primarily carrion, associated with bear-killed prey.

REPRODUCTION: The 40-day breeding season occurs in the late February-April period. Vixens are monestrous and their heat period is about two weeks long. The gestation period is 49 to 57 days and litters contain from 4 to 25 pups (usually about 11). When food is plentiful, breeding occurs early and litters usually are large. When food is scarce, breeding is delayed and litters are small and sometimes absent (resorbed). Both parents feed the young until weaning (about mid-August). The young are sexually mature at 9 to 10 months of age, and usually breed in their first year.

POPULATION STATUS: The arctic fox population is generally stable and abundant. However, its size is directly related to the availability of food which tends to be cyclic.

UTILIZATION: Arctic foxes usually are taken by trapping techniques. The harvest potential varies from about 140,000 to 160,000 animals depending on prey availability. Arctic fox harvests are limited by the vast, barren and inhospitable nature of the habitat. In recent years the North American (Alaska and Canada) harvest of arctic foxes has been about 40 to 50 thousand pelts valued at more than one million dollars annually.

REFERENCES

ANONYMOUS. 1978. Report on the Status of Canadian Wildlife Used by the Fur Industry. Dept. of Industry, Trade and Commerce, Ottawa. 66 pp.

_____. 1979. Fur Production, 1977-78. Statistics Canada, Ottawa. 17 pp.

BANFIELD, A.W.F. 1974. The Mammals of Canada. Univ. of Toronto Press. 438 pp.

COWAN, I. McTaggart, and C.J. Guiguet. 1965. The Mammals of British Columbia. Queens Printer, Victoria, B.C. 414 pp.

PETERSON, Randolph L. 1973. The Mammals of Eastern Canada. Oxford Univ. Press, Toronto. 465 pp.

SPELLER, S.W. 1977. Arctic Fox. Canadian Wildlife Service, Dept. of Fisheries and the Environment, Ottawa. 3 pp.

Map 7.   The Range of the Arctic Fox in the United States and Canada.

Fig. 7

The Management Status of the Arctic Fox in the United States and Canada

STATES, PROVINCES AND TERRITORIES	Present	Total Protection	Hunting Season	Trapping Season	Year-Round Harvesting	Limited Harvesting	Food Resource	Habitat Management	Population Inventories	Special Regulations	Private Lands Leased
United States											
Alabama											
Alaska	•		•	•		•					
Arizona											
Arkansas											
California											
Colorado											
Connecticut											
Delaware											
Florida											
Georgia											
Idaho											
Illinois											
Indiana											
Iowa											
Kansas											
Kentucky											
Louisiana											
Maine											
Maryland											
Massachusetts											
Michigan											
Minnesota											
Mississippi											
Missouri											
Montana											
Nebraska											
Nevada											
New Hampshire											
New Jersey											
New Mexico											
New York											
North Carolina											

STATES, PROVINCES AND TERRITORIES	Present	Total Protection	Hunting Season	Trapping Season	Year-Round Harvesting	Limited Harvesting	Food Resource	Habitat Management	Population Inventories	Special Regulations	Private Lands Leased
United States (Cont'd)											
North Dakota											
Ohio											
Oklahoma											
Oregon											
Pennsylvania											
Rhode Island											
South Carolina											
South Dakota											
Tennessee											
Texas											
Utah											
Vermont											
Virginia											
Washington											
West Virginia											
Wisconsin											
Wyoming											
Total (United States)	1	0	1	1	0	1	0	0	0	0	0
Canada											
Alberta	•			•		•				•	
British Columbia											
Manitoba	•			•		•			•	•	
New Brunswick											
Newfoundland	•			•		•					
Northwest Territories	•			•		•					
Nova Scotia											
Ontario	•			•		•			•		
Prince Edward Island											
Quebec	•				•						
Saskatchewan	•			•		•				•	
Yukon Territory	•			•		•				•	
Total (Canada)	8	0	0	7	1	7	0	0	2	4	0

RED FOX
(Vulpes vulpes)

DESCRIPTION: Red foxes are relatively small slender canids. Unlike domestic dogs, the red fox's foot pad is furred and oval shaped. The face and ears are long and pointed and the fur is long and silky. The red fox exhibits three major color phases: red, black (silver) and mixed (cross), as well as combinations of these color types. However, the red phase is the dominant color phase throughout the red fox's entire range. Red foxes have black feet, legs and backs of ears and a white-tipped bushy tail. The body fur usually is a reddish-yellow color that is darkest on the back, fading to a gray or white belly. The cross phase normally exhibits a dark band across the shoulders and another dark band down the middle of the back. These bands create a "cross" configuration on the pelt. The silver phase is primarily black with varying amounts of white-tipped guard hairs (silvering) usually on the face and haunches. Intermediate color phases exhibit a mixture of characteristics in two or more of the three major color phases. The proportion of each color phase in local populations changes in a gradient fashion from the southeastern states through Canada to Alaska. The cross and silver phases occur most often in northwestern North America and are relatively rare in the southeast. Two uncommon pelage phases also exist, "bastard" and "Samson" foxes. Bastard foxes are primarily brownish or buff in color and Samson foxes have few or no guard hairs. Adults reach 36 inches (92 cm) in total length (the tail accounts for ⅓ of the total length) and weigh 8 to 15 pounds (4-7 kg). Males are slightly larger than females. The skull has 42 teeth. There are 8 mammae.

HABITAT: The red fox is highly adaptable and occurs in a considerable range of habitats including southern agricultural lands, woodlots, prairies, ocean beaches, and alpine tundra. The highest red fox densities occur in relatively open agricultural areas interspersed with brushy areas, forested bluffs, woodlots and croplands.

FEEDING HABITS: The food items of the red fox are as varied as its habitat types. It is an opportunistic omnivore whose diet varies by season and habitat type. Meat is most prevalent in the diet during winter, often in the form of carrion, but invertebrates and vegetation frequently are eaten in snow-free periods and areas. Small mammals, the main prey, include moles, shrews, rats, mice, tree and ground squirrels, muskrats, ground hogs, rabbits and hares. Birds include ground nesting songbirds, pheasants, quail, grouse, ducks and sometimes wild turkey poults and domestic fowl. Invertebrates include beetles, grubs, caterpillars, grasshoppers, cicadas, crickets, and crayfish. Vegetation includes acorns, corn, grasses, sedges, seaweed, berries and other various succulent fruits. Occcasionally, red foxes eat frogs, snakes and fish.

BEHAVIOR: Red foxes tend to be nocturnal and crepuscular although they are active in the daytime during the whelping and pup-rearing period. A family social unit exists from the mating period until young are dispersed at about 6 months of age. During the remainder of the year red foxes essentially are solitary. They have an acute sense of smell and a keen sense of hearing. They often emit a hoarse, high-pitched bark when chasing prey such as rabbits and hares. The same barking sound is reportedly used by the red fox to "toll" hounds into a chase. It also is believed that red foxes enjoy being chased since they run longer distances than similar wild animals when chased, and utilize a wide variety of ingenious techniques for losing the hounds, rather than taking shelter in underground dens as do gray foxes. When capturing small mammals, red foxes exhibit a stiff-legged pounce on their prey. Red foxes are adept at stalking, rather than running down prey. They run in a smooth, effortless gait, appearing to float over the ground with their tails flowing straight out behind them. The trail consists of footprints in a neat, almost straight line, showing considerable foot drag in soft snow. In deep snow they tend to retrace their own trails, stepping in the same tracks each time.

REPRODUCTION: The peak breeding season for red foxes is mid-January to mid-March, with females being in estrus sometime during the December-March period. Females are monestrous and, although usually pursued by several males, pair bonding occurs after mating and a monogamous condition exists for several months. Gestation lasts from 51 to 53 days. Each litter contains 1 to 10 (average is 5) altricial pups. Pups are weaned at about one month of age and they begin to travel short distances from the den. Both parents care for the young until they become juveniles and begin to disperse at 14 to 16 weeks of age. Both sexes become sexually mature at about 10 months of age, and usually breed in the first year.

POPULATION STATUS: The North American red fox population appears to be generally stable. In boreal regions the populations appear to fluctuate in response to cyclic peaks in prey populations, while in open prairie areas there appear to be slight local declines in red fox numbers often in response to human pressures. Stable populations exhibit short term fluctuations in response to diseases, especially sarcoptic mange and rabies, and changes in prey availability and harvest efforts. Research conducted during the '70s has shown high pelt prices ($40-$80+) can increase harvest pressure and depress high populations.

UTILIZATION: Red foxes are pursued by trappers, consumptive hunters and "chasers" using many hounds. Pelts are taken by trappers and hunters but some houndsmen enjoy the chase only and do not attempt to kill the fox. Recent North American wild red fox harvests have yielded about 400 thousand pelts valued at more than 25 million dollars annually, making the red fox one of the premier North American furbearers.

REFERENCES

ANONYMOUS. 1978. Report of the Status of Canadian Wildlife Used by the Fur Industry. Revised ed. (1977). Department of Industry, Trade & Commerce, Ottawa, Canada, in Association with the Canada Fur Council.

BANFIELD, A.W.F. 1974. The Mammals of Canada. Univ. of Toronto Press. 438 pp.

BURT, W.H. 1954. The Mammals of Michigan. Univ. Mich. Press, Ann Arbor. 288 pp.
_____, and R. P. Grossenheider. 1976. A Field Guide to the Mammals. 3rd Edition. Houghton Mifflin Co., Boston. 289 pp.

DEEMS, E.F., and D. Pursley. 1978. North American Furbearers, Their Management, Research and Harvest Status in 1976. International Association of Fish and Wildlife Agencies. 171 pp.

GUNDERSON, H.L., and J.R. Beer. 1953. The Mammals of Minnesota. Univ. Minn. Press, Minneapolis. 190 pp.

HALL, E.R., and K.R. Kelson. 1959. Mammals of North America. Ronald Press Co., N.Y., New York. 1083 pp.

JONES, R.E., and R.J. Aulerich. 1981. Bibliography of Foxes. Journal Article No. 9871. Mich. Agr. Exp. Station. 141 pp.

PETERSON, Randolph L. 1966. The Mammals of Eastern Canada. Toronto, Oxford, University Press.

PILS, C.M., and M.A. Martin. 1978. Population Dynamics, Predator-Prey Relationships and Management of the Red Fox in Wisconsin. Wis. Dep. Nat. Res. Tech. Bull. No. 105. 56 pp.

SCOTT, T.G. 1955. An Evaluation of the Red Fox. Ill. Nat. Hist. Surv. Biol. Notes No. 35. 16 pp.

STORM, G.L., R.D. Andrews, R.L. Phillips, R.A. Bishop, D.B. Siniff, and J.R. Tester. 1976. Morphology, Reproduction, Dispersal, and Mortality of Midwestern Red Fox Populations. Wildl. Monogr. No. 49. 82 pp.

WALKER, E.P. 1975. Mammals of the World (third ed.). Johns Hopkins Press, Baltimore, Maryland. 1500 pp.

Map 8. **The Range of the Red Fox in the United States and Canada.**

Fig. 8 — The Management Status of the Red Fox in the United States and Canada

STATES, PROVINCES AND TERRITORIES	Present	Total Protection	Hunting Season	Trapping Season	Year-Round Harvesting	Limited Harvesting	Food Resource	Habitat Management	Population Inventories	Special Regulations	Private Lands Leased
United States											
Alabama	●		●	●		●				●	
Alaska	●		●	●		●					
Arizona											
Arkansas	●	●									
California	●	●									
Colorado	●		●	●		●					
Connecticut	●		●	●		●				●	
Delaware	●	●	●							●	
Florida	●	●									
Georgia	●		●	●		●			●	●	
Idaho	●		●	●	●	●				●	
Illinois	●		●	●		●			●	●	
Indiana	●		●	●		●			●		
Iowa	●		●	●		●			●	●	
Kansas	●		●	●		●					
Kentucky	●		●	●		●					
Louisiana	●		●	●			●				
Maine	●		●	●		●					
Maryland	●		●	●		●			●		
Massachusetts	●		●	●		●					
Michigan	●				●						
Minnesota	●		●	●		●			●	●	
Mississippi	●			●		●					
Missouri	●	●							●	●	
Montana	●				●						
Nebraska	●				●						
Nevada	●		●	●		●					
New Hampshire	●		●	●		●			●	●	
New Jersey	●		●			●			●	●	
New Mexico	●			●		●					
New York	●		●	●		●					
North Carolina	●		●			●					●
United States (Cont'd)											
North Dakota	●		●	●		●			●	●	●
Ohio	●		●	●							
Oklahoma	●		●	●		●			●		
Oregon	●			●	●						
Pennsylvania	●		●	●	●						
Rhode Island	●		●	●		●		●	●	●	
South Carolina	●		●	●		●	●		●	●	
South Dakota	●		●	●		●			●		
Tennessee	●	●							●	●	
Texas	●		●	●	●					●	
Utah	●				●						
Vermont	●		●	●							
Virginia	●		●	●		●			●		
Washington	●				●				●		
West Virginia	●		●	●		●					
Wisconsin	●		●	●		●			●		
Wyoming	●		●	●	●						
Total (United States)	48	6	35	35	10	31	1	1	19	16	2
Canada											
Alberta	●		●	●		●				●	
British Columbia	●		●	●	●						●
Manitoba	●			●		●			●	●	
New Brunswick	●		●	●					●		
Newfoundland	●			●		●					
Northwest Territories	●			●		●					
Nova Scotia	●		●	●							
Ontario	●		●	●	●				●		
Prince Edward Island	●		●	●		●				●	
Quebec	●		●	●	●						
Saskatchewan	●		●	●		●				●	
Yukon Territory	●			●		●				●	
Total (Canada)	12	0	8	12	3	7	0	0	3	5	1

GRAY FOX
(*Urocyon cinereoargenteus*)

DESCRIPTION: The gray fox is dog-like in appearance with an elongated, pointed muzzle, large pointed ears which are usually held erect and forward, moderately long legs, and a long heavily furred bushy tail. In general, the build of the gray fox is similar to that of the red fox, but it is distinguished by the grayish coloration, the median black stripe down its back and tail, the reddish-yellow sides of neck, back of ears, legs and feet, slightly smaller black-tipped tail (which is triangular in cross section), 3 pairs of teats compared to the red fox's 4 pairs, dark brown iris of eye and relatively coarse, wooly fur. The sexes are alike and no seasonal change in coloration occurs. Adult gray foxes are 35 to 44 inches (88 to 110 cm) in length and weigh from 5 to 14 pounds (2.3 to 6.2 kg). Gray fox skulls are readily distinguishable from those of red foxes. The post orbital process on a gray's skull is deep and distinct, while that of a red fox is shallow and indistinct. The gray fox skull has prominent paired ridges at the crest which join to form a U-shaped area at the posterior 1/3 of the skull. The crest of a red fox skull is smooth or only slightly ridged. Like the red fox the gray fox's skull has 42 teeth. There are 6 mammae.

HABITAT: The gray fox prefers wooded areas and brushlands. It does not inhabit open areas and prairies like the more adaptable red fox. Gray foxes are animals of warmer climates, hence in the northern part of their range they use dens for warmth during the winter months. Dens are located in hollow logs and trees, under rock piles, and occasionally in ground burrows. The dens are filled with grass, leaves or shredded bark.

FEEDING HABITS: The gray fox feeds on many of the same foods as the red fox. Small mammals constitute the bulk of the diet. Food items generally are determined by their availability. Rabbits and mice are the primary food items. Other wild mammals, small birds, and occasionally domestic livestock and poultry (often in the form of carrion) also are eaten. Insects, plants, fruits, berries and acorns are consumed during the summer and fall months. Surplus foods are sometimes cached for later consumption.

BEHAVIOR: The gray fox is considerably more secretive and cat-like in nature than the red fox. Grays are primarily nocturnal animals. They readily climb trees using their front feet to grasp the tree trunk and their hind feet to push upward. Gray foxes sun in trees and frequently take refuge there when pursued by dogs. Grays appear to be shier and less cunning than red foxes but when necessary they are fierce fighters. Under pen conditions gray foxes often kill red foxes. The gray fox can attain speeds of 26 to 28 miles per hour (42-45 kph) for short distances. It is a good swimmer. Gray foxes exhibit a yapping bark which usually is repeated 4 to 5 times in sucession and is louder and harsher than the bark of the red fox. Gray foxes also growl, squeal and chuckle.

REPRODUCTION: The breeding season of the gray fox extends from January to mid-May. The peak occurs from mid-February to mid-March. Most gray foxes breed during their first year. The gestation period varies from 51 to 63 days (average is 53 days). Females produce a single litter containing 1 to 10 young (average is 3 to 5) each year. The dark colored, scantily furred, blind newborn pups weigh only 3 ounces (85 g) each. Their eyes open at about 10 days of age. Young gray foxes leave their den at 3 months of age to hunt with their parents. The family breaks up in late summer.

POPULATION STATUS: Generally speaking, the gray fox population in North America is stable. But as man continues to clear woodlands for agriculture, commercial and private developments, gray fox habitats will decline. Unlike the red fox the gray fox is not susceptible to sarcoptic mange but, like the red fox, the gray fox is a major carrier of rabies, and in some locales this disease suppresses gray fox populations.

UTILIZATION: The gray fox provides considerable recreation to hunters, trappers and the fox-chasing public. Because of its habitats and secretive nature, trapping and hunting with dogs provide the best harvest opportunities. Gray fox fur is coarse and thin compared to the silkier and denser fur of the red fox and it is used primarily for trimmings and accessories. Gray fox pelts are less variable in color and value than those of the red fox and in recent years the annual market values of gray fox pelts ($30 to $50 each) has increased slowly but steadily. Recent national gray fox harvests have yielded 250 to 300 thousand pelts valued at 8 to 10 million dollars annually.

REFERENCES

BURT, W.H., and R.P. Grossenheider. 1964. A Field Guide to the Mammals. Houghton Mifflin Co., Boston. 289 pp.

DEEMS, E.F., and D. Pursley. 1978. North American Furbearers, Their Management, Research and Harvest Status in 1976. International Association of Fish and Wildlife Agencies. 171 pp.

HALL, E.R. 1981. The Mammals of North America. Vol. II. John Wiley & Sons, Inc. New York. 1181 pp.

SAMPSON, F.W., and W.O. Nagel. 1949. Controlling Coyote and Fox Damage on the Farm. Missouri Conservation Commission, Bulletin 18. 22 pp.

SEAGEARS, C.B. 1944. The Fox in New York. New York Conservation Depart. 85 pp.

SHELDON, W.G. 1949. Reproductive Behavior of Foxes in New York State. J. Mammal. 30: 236-246.

SCHWARTZ, C.W., and E.R. Schwartz. 1964. The Wild Mammals of Missouri. Univ. of Missouri Press and Missouri Conservation Commission, Kansas City. 341 pp.

SULLIVAN, E.G. 1956. Gray Fox Reproduction, Denning, Range, and Weights in Alabama. J. Mammal. 37: 346-351.

WOOD, J.E. 1958. Age Structure and Productivity of a Gray Fox Population. J. Mammal. 38: 74-86.

Map 9.   The Range of the Gray Fox in the United States and Canada.

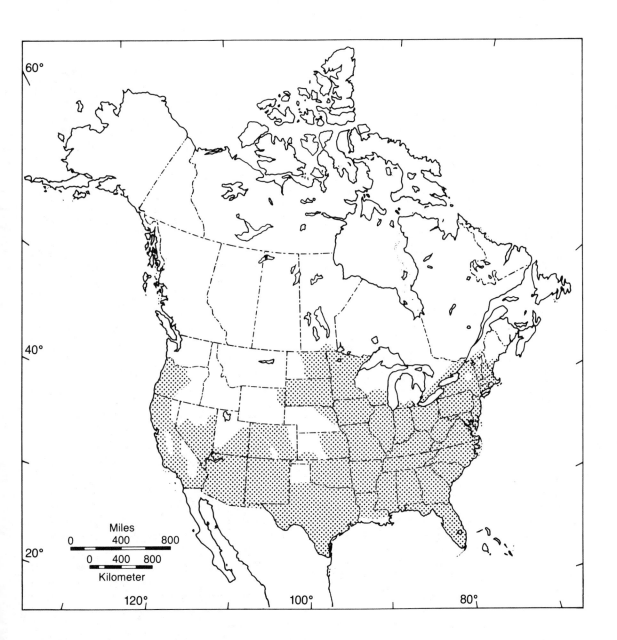

Fig. 9 **The Management Status of the Gray Fox in the United States and Canada**

STATES, PROVINCES AND TERRITORIES	Present	Total Protection	Hunting Season	Trapping Season	Year-Round Harvesting	Limited Harvesting	Food Resource	Habitat Management	Population Inventories	Special Regulations	Private Lands Leased
United States											
Alabama	●		●	●		●				●	
Alaska											
Arizona	●		●	●		●					
Arkansas	●		●	●		●					
California	●		●	●		●		●			
Colorado	●		●	●		●					
Connecticut	●		●	●		●				●	
Delaware	●				●						
Florida	●	●								●	
Georgia	●		●	●		●			●	●	
Idaho											
Illinois	●		●	●		●			●	●	
Indiana	●		●	●		●			●		
Iowa	●		●	●		●			●	●	
Kansas	●		●	●		●					
Kentucky	●		●	●	●						
Louisiana	●		●	●		●			●		
Maine	●		●	●		●					
Maryland	●		●	●		●			●		
Massachusetts	●		●	●		●					
Michigan	●				●						
Minnesota	●		●	●		●				●	
Mississippi	●			●		●					
Missouri	●		●	●					●	●	
Montana											
Nebraska	●				●						
Nevada	●		●	●		●			●		
New Hampshire	●		●	●		●			●	●	
New Jersey	●		●			●			●	●	
New Mexico	●			●		●					
New York	●		●	●		●					
North Carolina	●		●			●				●	●

STATES, PROVINCES AND TERRITORIES	Present	Total Protection	Hunting Season	Trapping Season	Year-Round Harvesting	Limited Harvesting	Food Resource	Habitat Management	Population Inventories	Special Regulations	Private Lands Leased
United States (Cont'd)											
North Dakota	●		●	●		●					
Ohio	●		●	●							
Oklahoma	●		●	●		●				●	
Oregon	●			●	●						
Pennsylvania	●		●	●	●						
Rhode Island	●		●	●		●			●	●	●
South Carolina	●		●	●		●	●			●	●
South Dakota	●		●	●	●						
Tennessee	●		●	●		●			●		
Texas	●		●	●	●					●	
Utah	●			●							
Vermont	●		●	●							
Virginia	●		●	●		●			●		
Washington											
West Virginia	●		●	●		●			●		
Wisconsin	●		●	●		●			●		
Wyoming	●		●	●	●						
Total (United States)	45	1	37	38	10	32	1	1	18	13	1
Canada											
Alberta											
British Columbia											
Manitoba											
New Brunswick											
Newfoundland											
Northwest Territories											
Nova Scotia											
Ontario	●			●	●				●		
Prince Edward Island											
Quebec											
Saskatchewan											
Yukon Territory											
Total (Canada)	1	0	0	1	1	0	0	0	1	0	0

BROWN BEAR
(*Ursus arctos*)

DESCRIPTION: Brown bears are large, stout-bodied animals with short tails and ears, "dished in" faces and non-retractable front claws which are large and adapted for digging. Hind claws are shorter than front claws. There are five well developed toes on each foot. Brown bears are distinguished by the large hump between their shoulders (at the withers). Pelage coloration is highly variable, ranging from pale yellow (blonde) to dark brown and nearly black. White hair tips give some bears a frosted or grizzled appearance. The sexes are similar in appearance and size, and young are similar to adults. Adults are 6 to 8 feet (1.8-2.4 m) in length and 325 to 1500 pounds (147-680 kg) in weight. Skull has 42 teeth. There are 6 mammae.

HABITAT: Brown bears live in alpine, subalpine and upper (montane) zones. They inhabit many vegetation communities from unbroken arctic tundra to unbroken timber (taiga), and from relatively dry areas to sea coast rain forests. Brown bears prefer areas with open meadows and mixed timber stands of conifers, aspen, alder and willow.

FEEDING HABITS: Brown bears generally are opportunistic omnivores that feed extensively on vegetation. They feed heavily on grasses, sedges, tuberous roots, berries and sometimes the cambium layer of trees. They also feed on carrion of large ungulates such as moose, caribou, deer, elk, cattle, horses and sheep; also small animals such as lemmings, mice, ground squirrels, ants, fish and wood-boring beetle larvae. Occasionally these bears kill and eat large ungulates.

BEHAVIOR: Brown bears tend to exhibit crepuscular activity periods, but they are known to move and feed in nocturnal and diurnal periods also. Home range may be 50 square miles (130 km²) but is usually much less. Males are more solitary than females and young. Several small family groups of females and young may be seen at one time in preferred feeding areas. Females exhibit strong defensive behavior around their cubs. Brown bears are territorial and they habitually use trails and rest areas around food sources. Their daily and seasonal movements are affected by temperature and food availability. Brown bears den from October to November and from March to April. These bears are bold and aggressive animals that should be avoided when possible. There are many historic accounts of unprovoked attacks, maulings and deaths as a result of human-brown bear encounters.

REPRODUCTION: Brown bears breed in the spring (usually May and June). They are promiscuous. Delayed implantation of 6 to 7 months is characteristic. A relatively short gestation period (around 60 days) follows implantation. From one to four cubs (usually 2) are born every third year. The sow exhibits a long period of parental care for the cubs, which nurse for up to 20 months. Cubs reach sexual maturity late, usually 5 to 7 years of age.

POPULATION STATUS: The brown bear formerly inhabited the midwest prairies and all of western North America to the Arctic. Its range now is limited to areas in and around Yellowstone Park, the mountains and forests of Idaho and Montana, northwestern Canada and Alaska. Wyoming, Montana, the Canadian provinces and Alaska report stable or increasing brown bear populations. Washington, Idaho and Utah report small remnant brown bear populations that appear to be hanging on. A grizzly bear was killed in Colorado in 1979. Subsequent research has not confirmed the presence of a population. The conservative management and protection programs that presently govern the hunting of brown bears should ensure a stable to increasing brown bear population in North America as long as sufficient habitats remain.

UTILIZATION: Limited brown bear hunting is allowed in Alaska, Yukon Territory, Northwest Territories, British Columbia, Alberta and Montana. There is some limited taking of brown bears for depredation control and human safety in Yellowstone and Glacier National Parks. Since brown bears are considered to be trophy animals there is little trade in hides, claws or other products, but in recent years brown bear hides have been sold for over $100 each and claws have sold for $40 each.

REFERENCES

ANTHONY, H.E. 1952. Animals of the World. Garden City Books, Garden City, New York. 354 pp.

ARMSTRONG, D.M. 1972. Distribution of Mammals in Colorado. Mus. of Nat. Hist., The Univ. of Kansas, Monogr. No. 3. 415 pp.

BARDACK, D. 1967. An Attack by a Grizzly Bear. J. Mammal. 48(3): 479.

BELTON, D. 1971. Grizzlies. Victoria. Nat. 28(2): 18-19.

BURT, W.H., and R. P. Grossenheider. 1964. A Field Guide to the Mammals. Houghton Mifflin Co., Boston. 284 pp.

CAUBLE, C. 1977. The Great Grizzly Grapple. Nat. Hist. 86(7): 74-81.

COLE, G.F. 1973. Management Involving Grizzly Bears in Yellowstone National Park, 1970-72. USDI Natl. Park Serv. Nat. Resource Rep. No. 7. 10 pp.

CRAIGHEAD, F.C., Jr. and J.J. Craighead. 1972. Grizzly Bear Prehibernation and Denning Activities as Determined by Radiotracking. Wildl. Monogr. No. 32. 35 pp.

CRAIGHEAD, J.J., M. Hornocker and F.C. Craighead, Jr. 1969. Reproductive Biology of Young Female Grizzly Bears. J. Reproduction & Fertility, suppl. 6. pp. 447-475.

_____, J.R. Varney, and F.C. Craighead, Jr. 1974. A Population Analysis of the Yellowstone Grizzly Bear. Mont. For. Conserv. Exp. Stn. Bulletin 40.

EBERTS, A. 1971. Grizzlies. Victoria. Nat. 28(4): 41-42.

FINEGAN, R.P. 1971. Grizzly Bear Harvests by Resident Hunters, 1965-70. Brit. Columbia Fish & Wildl. Branch. 63 pp.

GREER, K.R. 1972. Grizzly Bear Mortality and Management Programs in Montana During 1971. Montana Dept. Fish and Game, Job Comp. Rpt., Proj. W-120-R-3, No. L-1.1. 44 pp.

_____. 1974. Grizzly Bear Mortality and Management Programs in Montana during 1973. Montana Dept. Fish and Game, Job Compl. Rpt., Proj. W-120-R-5, No. L-1.1. 51 pp.

_____. 1976. Grizzly Bear Mortality and Management Programs in Montana during 1975. Montana Dept. Fish and Game, Job Compl. Rpt., Proj. W-120-R-7, No. L-1.1. 20 pp.

_____. 1977. Grizzly Bear Mortality and Management Programs in Montana during 1976. Montana Dept. Fish and Game, Job. Compl. Rpt., Proj. W-120-R-8, L-1.1. 20 pp.

HALL, E.R., and K.R. Kelson. 1959. The Mammals of North America. The Ronald

Press Company. 1083 pp.

HARDING, L.E., 1976. Den-site Characteristics of Arctic Coastal Grizzly Bears of Richards Islands, Northwest Territories, Canada. Can. J. Zool. 54(8): 1357-1363.

HERRERO, S. 1970. Man and the Grizzly Bear (Present, Past, but Future?). Bio. Science. 20(21): 1148-1153.

_____, and D. Hamer. 1977. Courtship and Copulation of a Pair of Grizzly Bears, w/ Comments on Reproduction, Plasticity and Strategy. J. Mammal. 58(3):441-444.

HORNOCKER, M.G. 1962. Population Characteristics and Social Reproduction Behavior of the Grizzly in Yellowstone Park. M.S. Thesis, Univ. Mont.

JOHNSON, A.S. 1973. Yellowstone's Grizzlies: Endangered or Prospering? Defenders of Wildl. New. reprint. pp. 557-568.

KLATSKE, R. 1969. The Grizzly Bear in Man's World. Wyo. Wildl. 33(1): 19-27.

KNIGHT, R.R., J. Basile, K. Greer, S. Judd, L. Oldenberg, and L. Roop. 1977. Yellowstone Grizzly Bear Investigations Annual Report of the Interagency Study Team 1976. Misc. Rpt. No. 10. 75 pp.

_____, et al. 1977. Yellowstone Grizzly Bear Investigations. U.S.D.I. National Park Service. pp. 1-107.

_____. 1978. Yellowstone Grizzly Bear Investigations. Annual Report of the Interagency Study Team 1977. Misc. Rpt. No. 11. 23 pp.

LAYSER. E.F. 1978. Grizzly Bears in the Southern Selkirk Mountains. Northwest Sci. 52(2): 77-91.

MARTINKA, C.J. 1971. Status and Management of Grizzly Bears in Glacier National Park, Montana. Trans. N.A. Wildl. and Mgmt. Res. Conf. 36: 312-322.

_____. 1974. Population Characteristics of Grizzly Bears in Glacier National Park, Montana. J. Mammal. 55(1): 21-29.

_____. 1974. Preserving the Natural Status of Grizzlies in Glacier National Park. Wildl. Soc. Bull. 2(1): 13-17.

MEALEY, S.P., C.J. Jonkel and R. Demarchi. 1977. Habitat Criteria for Grizzly Bear Management. Int. Congr. Game Biol. 13: 276-289.

MOMENT, G.B. 1970. Man-Grizzly Problems — Past and Present/Implications for Endangered Species. Bio. Science. 20(21): 1142-1144.

MUNDY, K.R.D., and D.R. Flock. 1973. Background for Managing Grizzly Bears in the National Parks of Canada. Can. Wildl. Serv. Rep. Serv. No. 22. 34 pp.

PEARSON, A.M. 1970. Population Characteristics of the Northern Interior Grizzly in the Yukon Territory, Canada. Int. Congr. Game Biol. 9: 370-374.

_____. 1975 The Northern Interior Grizzly Bear (Ursus arctos). Canadian Wildl. Serv. Rpt. Series No. 34. 86 pp.

ROOP, L. 1976. Grizzly Bear. Wyoming Game and Fish Dept., Job Compl. Rpt. Proj. W-87-R-2. 64 pp.

SCHMIDT, J., and D.L. Gilbert. 1978. Big Game of North America, Ecology and Management. Wildlife Mgmt. Institute. 494 pp.

STEBLER, A.M. 1970. Man and the Grizzly — Coexistence? Intro Bio. Science. 20(21): 1141.

STIRLING, I., A.M. Pearson and F.L. Bunnell. 1976. Population Ecology Studies of Polar and Grizzly Bears in Northern Canada. Trans. N. Am. Wildl. Conf. 41: 421-430.

STUART, T.J. 1978. Management Models for Human Use of Grizzly Bear Habitat.

Trans. N. Am. Wildl. Nat. Resource. Conf. 43: 433-441.

TROYER, W.A. 1962. Size, Distribution, Structure, and Harvest of a Kodiak Bear Population. M.S. Thesis, Univ. Mont. 48 pp.

Map 10. The Range of the Brown Bear in the United States and Canada.

Fig. 10 **The Management Status of the Brown Bear in the United States and Canada**

STATES, PROVINCES AND TERRITORIES	Present	Total Protection	Hunting Season	Trapping Season	Year-Round Harvesting	Limited Harvesting	Food Resource	Habitat Management	Population Inventories	Special Regulations	Private Lands Leased
United States											
Alabama											
Alaska	●		●			●	●		●		
Arizona											
Arkansas											
California											
Colorado		●									
Connecticut											
Delaware											
Florida											
Georgia											
Idaho	●	●									
Illinois											
Indiana											
Iowa											
Kansas											
Kentucky											
Louisiana											
Maine											
Maryland											
Massachusetts											
Michigan											
Minnesota											
Mississippi											
Missouri											
Montana	●		●			●		●	●	●	
Nebraska											
Nevada											
New Hampshire											
New Jersey											
New Mexico											
New York											
North Carolina											
United States (Cont'd)											
North Dakota											
Ohio											
Oklahoma											
Oregon											
Pennsylvania											
Rhode Island											
South Carolina											
South Dakota											
Tennessee											
Texas											
Utah											
Vermont											
Virginia											
Washington	●	●									
West Virginia											
Wisconsin											
Wyoming	●	●									
Total (United States)	5	4	2	0	0	2	1	1	2	1	0
Canada											
Alberta	●		●			●	●			●	
British Columbia	●		●			●	●				
Manitoba											
New Brunswick											
Newfoundland											
Northwest Territories	●		●			●	●		●		
Nova Scotia											
Ontario											
Prince Edward Island											
Quebec											
Saskatchewan											
Yukon Territory	●		●			●	●		●		
Total (Canada)	4	0	4	0	0	4	4	0	2	1	0

96

BLACK BEAR
(*Ursus americanus*)

DESCRIPTION: The black bear is the smallest of the North American bears. The pelage color varies from black in the east to black and brown phases in the west. Black bears may have a small white patch on their chest. The sexes are similar in appearance although males usually are larger. Adults are 5-6 feet (1.5-1.8 mm) long. Yearlings weigh about 60 pounds (27 kg), while adults weigh from 100 to over 400 pounds (45-181 kg). The skull has 42 teeth. There are 6 mammae.

HABITAT: Black bears occur in heavily forested areas, including large swamps and/or mountainous areas. Mixed hardwood forests interspersed with streams and swamps are typical habitats.

FEEDING HABITS: Black bears are omnivorous, foraging on a wide variety of plants and animals. Typical foods include grasses, wood fiber, berries, nuts, tubers, insects, small mammals, eggs, carrion and garbage. Bears rarely starve, but reproductive failures occur following years with poor mast (berry and nut) crops.

BEHAVIOR: Black bears are typically nocturnal although they occasionally are active during the day. They are basically solitary animals that live in large (several square miles) territories. In the south, black bears tend to be active year-round, but in northern areas, black bears undergo a period of semi-hibernation during winter. In this period of dormancy, bears use dens, such as hollow logs, windfalls, brush piles and caves. The territorial behavior of bears limits the maximum number of the species that can occupy an area. Larger bears will kill and eat smaller ones. Bears are not compatible with agriculture, some forestry practices, recreation areas or urbanization. Occasionally, black bears destroy apiaries, livestock and trees (while feeding on the inner bark). Bears also become a nuisance when they forage in garbage dumps or rummage through vacation homes and campsites.

REPRODUCTION: Black bears breed during the summer months, usually in late June or early July. Delayed implantation occurs and the embryo is not implanted until the winter dormancy period. Bears are polygamous and males travel extensively in search of receptive females. Fighting occurs between rival males as well as males and unreceptive females. Dominant females may suppress the breeding activities of subordinate females. Parturition occurs in January or February. Litters usually contain 2 or 3 cubs that weigh 7 to 12 ounces (198-340 g) at birth. After parturition the sow may continue her winter sleep while the cubs are awake and nursing. Lactating females do not come into estrus, so generally they only breed every other year. Parental care is solely the female's responsibility. Males will kill and eat cubs if given the opportunity. Cubs are weaned in late summer but usually remain close to the female throughout their first year. This social unit breaks up when the female comes into her next estrus. After the breeding season, the female and her yearlings may travel together for a few weeks. Black bears become sexually mature at approximately 3 1/2 years of age, but some females may not breed until their fourth year or later.

POPULATION STATUS: Black bear population levels appear to be directly related to the amount of habitat, which is relatively stable in North America. Habitat loss is causing local declines in some areas, while habitat improvement is causing local increases in others.

UTILIZATION: The black bear is taken most often as a game or nuisance animal rather than a furbearer. It is harvested for its meat, claws and gall bladder, as well as for trophy values. Pelts are used in mounts, rugs and certain hats, while claws are used for jewery and gall bladders for medicinal and aphrodisiac purposes. In recent years the market value of black bear pelts has been about $50, while that for claws has been $2 to $3 each and for gall bladders about $45.

REFERENCES

BURT, W. H. 1954. The Mammals of Michigan. University of Michigan Press, Ann Arbor. 228 pp.

———, and R.P. Grossenheider. 1976. A Field Guide to the Mammals. 3rd Edition. Houghton Mifflin Co., Boston. 289 pp.

DEEMS, E.F., and D. Pursley. 1978. North American Furbearers, Their Management, Research and Harvest Status in 1976. International Association Fish & Wildlife Agencies. 171 pp.

GUNDERSON, H.L. and J.R. Beer. 1953. The Mammals of Minnesota. Univ. Minn. Press, Minneapois. 190 pp.

LINDZEY, J.S. and Mezlow. 1976. Home Range and Habitat Use of Black Bears in Washington. J. Wildl. Manage. 41(3)

POELKER, R.J. and H.D. Hartwell. 1976. The Black Bear of Washington. Wash. State Game Dept. Biol. Bull. No. 14. 180 pp.

Map 11. The Range of the Black Bear in the United States and Canada.

Fig. 11   **The Management Status of the Black Bear in the United States and Canada**

STATES, PROVINCES AND TERRITORIES	Present	Total Protection	Hunting Season	Trapping Season	Year-Round Harvesting	Limited Harvesting	Food Resource	Habitat Management	Population Inventories	Special Regulations	Private Lands Leased
United States											
Alabama	●	●									
Alaska	●		●		●	●	●		●		
Arizona	●		●			●	●			●	●
Arkansas	●	●									
California	●		●			●	●		●		
Colorado	●		●			●				●	
Connecticut	●	●									
Delaware											
Florida	●		●			●	●	●	●	●	
Georgia	●		●			●	●	●	●	●	
Idaho	●		●		●	●	●		●		
Illinois											
Indiana											
Iowa											
Kansas											
Kentucky	●	●									
Louisiana	●		●			●			●		
Maine	●		●	●		●	●			●	●
Maryland	●	●									
Massachusetts	●		●			●	●			●	
Michigan	●		●			●	●	●	●	●	
Minnesota	●		●			●	●	●		●	
Mississippi	●	●									
Missouri	●	●									
Montana	●		●				●		●		
Nebraska											
Nevada	●	●									
New Hampshire	●		●			●	●		●		
New Jersey	●	●									
New Mexico	●		●			●			●		
New York	●		●			●	●		●	●	
North Carolina	●		●			●		●			
United States (Cont'd)											
North Dakota											
Ohio		●									
Oklahoma	●	●									
Oregon	●		●			●	●				
Pennsylvania	●		●			●	●		●		
Rhode Island											
South Carolina	●		●			●	●	●	●	●	
South Dakota	●	●									
Tennessee	●		●			●	●	●	●	●	●
Texas	●	●									
Utah	●		●			●					
Vermont	●		●			●	●		●	●	
Virginia	●		●			●	●	●	●	●	
Washington	●		●			●	●				
West Virginia	●		●			●	●	●	●		
Wisconsin	●		●			●	●	●	●	●	
Wyoming	●		●			●			●		
Total (United States)	40	13	28	1	2	27	22	10	22	14	1
Canada											
Alberta	●		●			●	●			●	
British Columbia	●		●			●	●				
Manitoba	●		●	●		●	●		●	●	
New Brunswick	●		●			●	●		●		
Newfoundland	●		●			●	●				
Northwest Territories	●		●		●	●	●				
Nova Scotia	●		●	●		●	●			●	
Ontario	●		●	●		●	●				
Prince Edward Island											
Quebec	●		●	●		●	●		●	●	
Saskatchewan	●		●	●		●	●			●	
Yukon Territory	●		●			●	●		●		
Total (Canada)	11	0	11	5	1	11	11	0	4	5	0

POLAR BEAR
(*Ursus maritimus*)

DESCRIPTION: Polar bears are distinctively large whitish animals with long necks and small narrow heads with small ears. The pelage color is creamy white in winter and yellowish white in summer. Adults reach 5 to 10 feet (150-300 cm) in length and weigh 551 to 1,545 pounds (250-700 kg). Adult males average 992 pounds (450 kg) and females about 705 pounds (320 kg). The skull has 42 teeth. There are 6 mammae.

HABITAT: Polar bears primarily are marine mammals. They frequent the arctic coastlines and pack ice in a circumpolar distribution. They tend to avoid solidly frozen sea ice and open seas. Denning areas usually are inshore and occasionally young bears travel many miles (several hundred kilometers) inland.

FEEDING HABITS: The polar bear has an extremely variable diet. Seals are the primary food item and carrion is a major food source. Marine food items include fish, walrus, seabirds and invertebrates. Land food items include reindeer, caribou, musk-ox, arctic hares, birds, eggs, vegetation and berries.

BEHAVIOR: Polar bears wander continuously in the Arctic ecosystem. The only exceptions are females and their cubs during the denning period and those bears that congregate in coastline "staging" sites prior to ice formation. Polar bears are unpredictable in their behavior toward man and they have been known to stalk and kill humans.

REPRODUCTION: Polar bears become sexually mature as 5 to 7 years of age. Mating takes place in April or May and implantation is delayed. Adult females are only in an estrus condition every other year since lactating females (mothers nursing cubs) do not have an estrus period. Females are polyandrous and pairing only occurs for a 2 to 3 week period. Pregnant females move inshore during early winter to dig an overwintering hibernaculum (den) in icy ridges or snow banks. Parturition occurs between November and early January after a 228 to 254 day gestation period. Litters contain from 1 to 4 cubs (the average is 2). The cubs are naked and blind at birth. Their first coat is white and wooly and their eyes open at about six weeks of age. Mother and young emerge from the den about March. Cubs stay with their mother until their second summer when they are driven off as the female enters her next estrus (breeding condition).

POPULATION STATUS: In North America, and worldwide, polar bear populations are stable to slightly increasing. World population estimates are in the vicinity of 10,000 animals. Approximately 600 to 1,000 of these bears occur in northern Manitoba where the Owl River polar bear denning area, thought to be the largest in the world, produces about 150 young annually.

UTILIZATION: Sport hunting for polar bears is virtually nonexistent although some native quotas include limited opportunities for transfer of hunting rights in guide situations. Most polar bears harvested in North America are taken by Innuit hunters although several bears are shot each year in community protection programs. The worldwide management of the polar bear resource varies from quota restrictions to total protection. Polar bears pelts generally bring less than $1,000 each but some have sold for as much as $3,000. In North America the annual harvest is approximately 500 polar bears and the average pelt market value is $500 to $700.

REFERENCES

ANONYMOUS. Fur Production, Season 1977-1978. Statistics Canada. May 1979. Ottawa, Ontario.

_____. Report of the Status of Canadian Wildlife Used by the Fur Industry, Revised Edition (1977). Department of Industry, Trade & Commerce, Ottawa, Canada, in association with the Canada Fur Council.

BANFIELD, A.W.F. 1974. The Mammals of Canada. University of Toronto Press. 438 pp.

BURT, W.H., and R.P. Grossenheider. 1964. A Field Guide to the Mammals. Houghton Mifflin Company, Boston. 289 pp.

HALL, E.R., and K.R. Kelson. 1959. Mammals of North America. Ronald Press Co., N.Y., New York. 1083 pp.

PETERSON, Randolph L. 1966. The Mammals of Eastern Canada. Toronto, Oxford University Press.

WALKER, E.P. 1975. Mammals of the World (third ed.). Johns Hopkins Press, Baltimore, Maryland. 1500 pp.

Map 12.   The Range of the Polar Bear in the United States
and Canada.

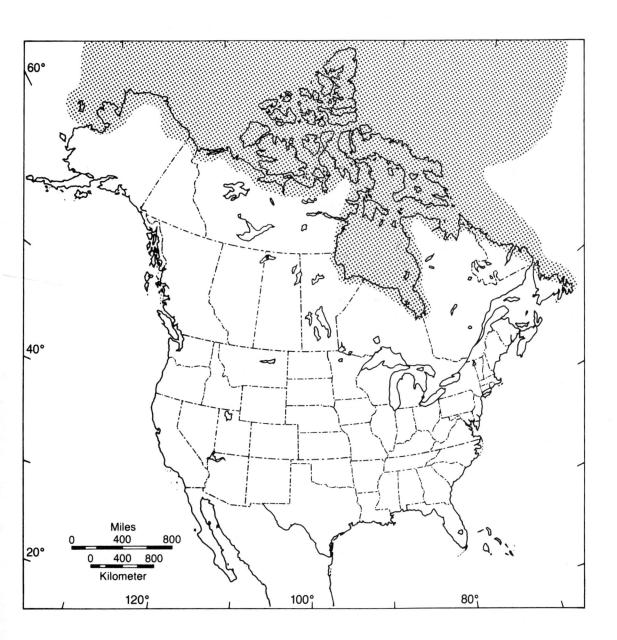

Fig. 12 **The Management Status of the Polar Bear in the United States and Canada**

STATES, PROVINCES AND TERRITORIES	Present	Total Protection	Hunting Season	Trapping Season	Year-Round Harvesting	Limited Harvesting	Food Resource	Habitat Management	Population Inventories	Special Regulations	Private Lands Leased
United States											
Alabama											
Alaska	●		●			●			●		
Arizona											
Arkansas											
California											
Colorado											
Connecticut											
Delaware											
Florida											
Georgia											
Idaho											
Illinois											
Indiana											
Iowa											
Kansas											
Kentucky											
Louisiana											
Maine											
Maryland											
Massachusetts											
Michigan											
Minnesota											
Mississippi											
Missouri											
Montana											
Nebraska											
Nevada											
New Hampshire											
New Jersey											
New Mexico											
New York											
North Carolina											

STATES, PROVINCES AND TERRITORIES	Present	Total Protection	Hunting Season	Trapping Season	Year-Round Harvesting	Limited Harvesting	Food Resource	Habitat Management	Population Inventories	Special Regulations	Private Lands Leased
United States (Cont'd)											
North Dakota											
Ohio											
Oklahoma											
Oregon											
Pennsylvania											
Rhode Island											
South Carolina											
South Dakota											
Tennessee											
Texas											
Utah											
Vermont											
Virginia											
Washington											
West Virginia											
Wisconsin											
Wyoming											
Total (United States)	1	0	1	0	0	1	0	0	1	0	0
Canada											
Alberta											
British Columbia											
Manitoba	●	●				●			●		
New Brunswick											
Newfoundland	●	●									
Northwest Territories	●		●			●	●		●	●	
Nova Scotia											
Ontario	●					●	●				
Prince Edward Island											
Quebec	●		●			●	●		●	●	
Saskatchewan											
Yukon Territory	●		●			●	●		●	●	
Total (Canada)	6	2	3	0	0	5	4	0	4	3	0

BASSARISK
(*Bassariscus astutus*)

DESCRIPTION: Bassarisks, commonly called "ringtails", are small, slender, catlike animals with small triangular heads, huge round-tipped ears and disproportionately large eyes. Their tails are brownish-black with seven white rings and a black tip. The black rings are not complete on the underside of the tail. The tail comprises slightly more than one-half of the total length. Adults are 25 to 31 inches (64-79 cm) in length and weigh 2 to 2 1/2 pounds (0.9-1.1 kg). Sexes are alike, but females usually are slightly smaller than males. Ringtails have five toes on each foot, thick fur between the footpads and semi-retractile claws. The skull has 40 teeth. There are 4 mammae.

HABITAT: The bassarisk inhabits grasslands, woodlands, chaparral, mesquite and cactus plains from coastal areas to 9,000-foot mountain ranges. It shelters and dens in rock crevices, mine shafts, cabins and under boulders in dry creek beds, and in hollow logs and trees.

FEEDING HABITS: Ringtails are opportunistic omnivores. They eat insects, spiders, small mammals and reptiles, birds, berries, fruits, nuts, carrion, and an occasional amphibian.

BEHAVIOR: Bassarisks are almost entirely nocturnal and quite secretive. These agile animals are able to climb vertical crevices and rough walls. Their ability to rotate their hind feet in a 180-degree angle permits them to descend vertical surfaces head-first. Adults usually are solitary except during the mating season. Vocalizations include a coughing fox-like bark, a whine, a long, plaintive, raccoon-like, high-pitched wail and a staccato chittering, especially common during the mating season. Ringtails habitually defecate on rocks, logs and tree limbs. They also scent-mark such places with urine, and their anal glands emit a sweetish, musky odor.

REPRODUCTION: The breeding season is March and April. From one to five (usually 3 or 4) altricial young are born after a 51 to 53 day gestation period. The newborns weigh slightly over an ounce (29 gm) and resemble small kittens. The female drives the adult male from the nest area before the young are born.

POPULATION STATUS: The ringtail is most abundant in southern Arizona, New Mexico and southwestern Texas, where its preferred habitats occur. Although its populations are relatively stable in California, it is less abundant in Nevada and Utah. The ringtail's range becomes marginal in Oregon, Wyoming, Oklahoma and Arkansas where the animal is scarce.

UTILIZATION: The ringtail is a very important furbearer in Texas. About 80,000 pelts are marketed annually for a total value of over $500,000. The annual harvests are much smaller in Arizona and New Mexico, and only a few ringtails are taken in the remainder of their range.

REFERENCES

BAILEY, E.P. 1974. Notes on the Development, Mating Behavior, and Vocalization of Captive Ringtails. The Southwestern Naturalist. 19(1): 117-119.

BURT, W.H., and R.P. Grossenheider. 1964. A Field Guide to the Mammals. Houghton Mifflin Co., Boston. 289 pp.

CAHALANE, V.H. 1954. Mammals of North America. The MacMillan Co., N.Y.

CARAS, R.A. 1967. North American Mammals: Fur-bearing Animals of the United States and Canada. Meredith Press, N.Y.

DEEMS, E.F. and D. Pursley. 1978. North American Furbearers, Their Management, Research and Harvest Status in 1976. International Association of Fish and Wildlife Agencies. 171 pp.

HALL, E.R., and K.R. Kelson. 1959. The Mammals of North America. Ronald Press Co., N.Y.

POGLAYEN-NEUWALL, I., and I. Poglayen-Neuwall. 1980. Gestation Period and Parturition of the Ringtail Bassariscus Astutus (Liechtenstein, 1830). Zeitschrift fur Saugetierkunde. 45(2): 73-81.

SEALANDER, J.A., and P.S. Gipson. 1972. The Southwestern Naturalist. 16(3 & 4): 458-459.

SETON, E.T. 1929. Lives of Game Animals. Vol. 11, Part 1. Doubleday, Doran and Co., Inc., N.Y.

TAYLOR, W.P. 1954. Food Habits and Notes on Life History of the Ringtailed Cat in Texas. Journal of Mammalogy. 35(1): 55-63.

TOWEILL, D.E., and J.G. Teer. 1977. Food Habits of Ringtails in the Edwards Plateau Region of Texas. Journal of Mammalogy. 58(4): 660-663.

TRAPP, G.R. 1978. Comparative Behavioral Ecology of the Ringtail and Gray Fox in Southwestern Utah. Carnivore. 1(2): 3-32.

WALKER, E.P. 1975. Mammals of the World. 3rd ed. Johns Hopkins Univ. Press, Baltimore.

Map 13.   **The Range of the Bassarisk in the United States and Canada.**

Fig. 13

The Management Status of the Bassarisk in the United States and Canada

STATES, PROVINCES AND TERRITORIES	Present	Total Protection	Hunting Season	Trapping Season	Year-Round Harvesting	Limited Harvesting	Food Resource	Habitat Management	Population Inventories	Special Regulations	Private Lands Leased
United States											
Alabama											
Alaska											
Arizona	●		●	●		●				●	
Arkansas											
California	●	●							●		
Colorado	●			●		●					
Connecticut											
Delaware											
Florida											
Georgia											
Idaho											
Illinois											
Indiana											
Iowa											
Kansas											
Kentucky											
Louisiana	●			●		●					
Maine											
Maryland											
Massachusetts											
Michigan											
Minnesota											
Mississippi											
Missouri											
Montana											
Nebraska											
Nevada	●	●									
New Hampshire											
New Jersey											
New Mexico	●			●		●					
New York											
North Carolina											

STATES, PROVINCES AND TERRITORIES	Present	Total Protection	Hunting Season	Trapping Season	Year-Round Harvesting	Limited Harvesting	Food Resource	Habitat Management	Population Inventories	Special Regulations	Private Lands Leased
United States (Cont'd)											
North Dakota											
Ohio											
Oklahoma	●										
Oregon	●	●									
Pennsylvania											
Rhode Island											
South Carolina											
South Dakota											
Tennessee											
Texas	●		●	●	●					●	●
Utah	●				●						
Vermont											
Virginia											
Washington											
West Virginia											
Wisconsin											
Wyoming	●				●						
Total (United States)	11	3	2	5	3	4	0	0	1	2	1
Canada											
Alberta											
British Columbia											
Manitoba											
New Brunswick											
Newfoundland											
Northwest Territories											
Nova Scotia											
Ontario											
Prince Edward Island											
Quebec											
Saskatchewan											
Yukon Territory											
Total (Canada)	0	0	0	0	0	0	0	0	0	0	0

RACCOON
(*Procyon lotor*)

DESCRIPTION: The raccoon is perhaps the most widely recognized furbearer in North America. Raccoons or "coons" as they often are called, are easily distinguished by their black mask and ringed tail. They have black markings on their face, tail and feet. The pelage ranges in color from gray with a reddish or "rusty" tint to a medium gray or silver with a blackish tint. The tail rings vary in color from reddish-gray to silver, alternating with black. Albinos may occur but are rare. Males and females are marked alike. Males are slightly larger than females but the difference often is indistinct. The total body length of adult raccoons ranges from 25 to 35 inches (64-89 cm) including a 6 to 12 inch (15-31 cm) tail. In marginal habitats or overpopulated areas, the average weight of adult males may be 9 to 10 pounds (4-4.5 kg) while females average 8 to 9 pounds (3.6-4.0 kg). In good habitats the average weight of adult males and females may be as high as 13 to 16 pounds (6-7 kg) respectively. Captive raccoons may weigh as much as 45 pounds (20 kg). The skull has 40 teeth. There are 6 mammae.

HABITAT: Raccoons are extremely adaptable and they occur in a wide variety of habitats. While the preferred habitats are coastal wetlands and river drainage systems associated with woodlands and farmlands, raccoons may be found in upland forests, suburban housing developments and parks.

FEEDING HABITS: The raccoon's diet is variable. When food is abundant raccoons apparently prefer foods with high sugar content, but when food is scarce raccoons forage oportunistically. In forested or upland regions, plant foods such as acorns, fruits, berries and cultivated crops comprise 50 to 80 percent of the diet. The remaining 20 to 50 percent consists largely of insects and crayfish. In wetland areas raccoons feed primarily on animal matter, especially aquatic invertebrates. Raccoons are considered to be significant predators of nesting animals, especially waterfowl. In certain areas raccoon depredations of waterfowl, wild turkey and sea turtle eggs have limited the reproductive success of these species. Crop depredation and predation on domestic fowl by raccoons is a serious problem to some farmers. Raccoons frequently raid trash cans and food left unattended in parks, suburbs and urban areas.

BEHAVIOR: Raccoons are nocturnal and seldom active in the daytime. Raccoons that appear to be sleeping or resting in the open or wandering aimlessly in daylight hours should not be approached since they may carry diseases (including rabies) that are infectious to humans and many domestic animals. Raccoons do not hibernate but they may be inactive for periods of several days during severe winter weather. They usually den or "hole up" in hollow trees but hollow logs, ground burrows, rock crevices, chimneys, attics and barnlofts also are used.

REPRODUCTION: In the northern portion of the raccoon's North American range the breeding season is January through March (peak is February). In southern areas the breeding season usually is later, but births have occurred throughout the year. Gestation is approximately 63 days and parturition usually occurs in April and May. Litters contain 2 to 6 altricial young and litter sizes tend to be smaller in the southern portion of its range than in the north. Raccoons do not mate for life but males usually remain with the

117

females from breeding to parturition, and sometimes the male assists in rearing the young. The young are weaned at about 3 months of age. Females may reach sexual maturity and breed during their first year but males generally do not become sexually mature until their second year.

POPULATION STATUS: Raccoons have become more numerous since the turn of the century. They have adapted to urbanization and are becoming increasingly common in urban and suburban areas. Population densities range from one raccoon per acre to one per 100 acres or more, depending on habitat quality.

UTILIZATION: Raccoon pelts and meat have been continually harvested by both hunters and trappers since the colonial period even though market values for raccoon fur have fluctuated widely. During the late 1920s, raccoon coats became popular and "coon" pelt prices rose to an unprecedented $14 average. By the late 1950s the market value for raccoon pelts had declined to about a $1 average. In 1970 the average market value of a raccoon pelt was $3.50 but by 1976 the average value was a new unprecedented high of $26. In recent years the average annual North American raccoon harvest has stablized at about 4 million pelts while the total annual market values have fluctuated between 90 and 100 million dollars.

REFERENCES

ANONYMOUS. 1959. Fur Animals of Indiana. Indiana Dept. of Cons., Division of Fish and Game, Pittman-Robertson Bull. No. 4.

ATKESON, T.Z., and D.C. Hulse. 1953. Trapping Versus Night Hunting for Controlling Raccoons and Opossums within Sanctuaries. J. Wildl. Manage. 17(2): 159-162.

BUTTERFIELD, R.T. 1944. Populations, Hunting Pressure, and Movement of Ohio Raccoons. Trans N. Am. Wildl. Conf. 9: 337-344

CUNNINGHAM, E.R. 1962. A Study of the Eastern Raccoon *(Procyon lotor)* the Atomic Energy Commission Savannah River Plant. M.S. Thesis, Univ. of Georgia, Athens.

DAVIS, J.R. 1959. A Preliminary Progress Report on Nest Predation as a Limiting Factor in Wild Turkey Populations. Proc. Natl. Wild Turkey Symp. S.E. Sect. The Wildl. Soc. 1: 138-145.

DORNEY, R.S. 1954. Ecology of Marsh Raccoons. J. Wildl. Mange. 18(2): 217-225.

ERICKSON, A.B., and H.I. Scudder. 1947. The Raccoon as a Predator on Turtles. J. Mammal. 28(4): 406-407.

JOHNSON, A.S. 1970. Biology of the Raccoon *(Procyon lotor varius). Bull. 402. Agricultural Experiment Station, Auburn Univ., Auburn, Alabama. 148 pp.*

MECH, L.D., D.M. Barnes and J.R. Tester. 1968. Seasonal Weight Changes, Mortality, and Population Structure of Raccoons in Minnesota. J. Mammal. 49(1): 63-73.

———, J.R. Tester and D.W. Warner. 1966. Fall Daytime Resting Habits of Raccoons as Determined by Telemetry. J. Mammal. 47(3): 450-466.

NETTLES, V.F., J.H. Shaddock, R.K. Sikes and C.R. Reyes. 1979. Rabies in Translocated Raccoons. Am. J. Publ. Health. 69:601-602.

SANDERSON, G.C. 1951. Breeding Habits and a History of the Missouri Raccoon Population from 1941 to 1948. Trans. N. Am. Wildl. Conf. 16: 445-461.

118

SAVAGE, W.N. 1977. Fur Facts from Long Ago. Fur-Fish-Game. 73(5): 46-49.

SIKES, R.K. 1973. Rabies. Pages 3-9 Infectious Diseases of Wild Mammals. J.W. Davis, L.H. Karstad, and D.O. Trainer. Iowa State Univ. Press, Ames, Iowa.

TWICHELL, A.R., and H.H. Dill. 1949. One Hundred Raccoons from One Hundred and Two Acres. J. Mammal. 30(2): 130-133.

TYSON, E.L. 1950. Summer Food Habits of the Raccoon in Southwest Washington. J. Mammal. 31(4): 448-449.

Map 14. **The Range of the Raccoon in the United States and Canada.**

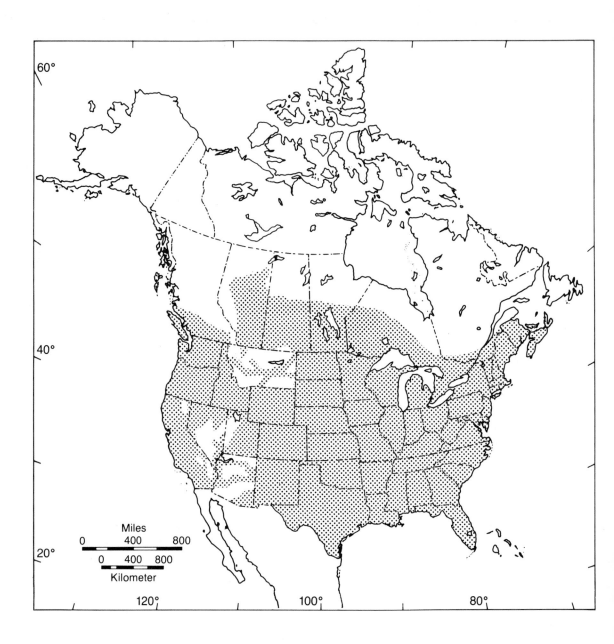

Fig. 14

The Management Status of the Raccoon in the United States and Canada

STATES, PROVINCES AND TERRITORIES	Present	Total Protection	Hunting Season	Trapping Season	Year-Round Harvesting	Limited Harvesting	Food Resource	Habitat Management	Population Inventories	Special Regulations	Private Lands Leased
United States											
Alabama	●		●	●		●	●			●	
Alaska	●		●	●	●						
Arizona	●		●	●		●				●	
Arkansas	●		●	●		●	●				
California	●		●	●		●	●				
Colorado	●		●	●	●						
Connecticut	●		●	●		●	●			●	
Delaware	●		●	●			●				●
Florida	●				●		●			●	
Georgia	●		●	●		●	●			●	
Idaho	●		●	●	●	●					
Illinois	●		●	●		●	●		●	●	
Indiana	●		●	●		●	●	●	●		
Iowa	●		●	●		●	●		●	●	
Kansas	●		●	●		●	●			●	
Kentucky	●		●	●		●					
Louisiana	●		●	●	●	●	●			●	
Maine	●		●	●		●	●			●	
Maryland	●		●	●		●	●		●	●	●
Massachusetts	●		●	●		●	●			●	
Michigan	●		●	●		●	●				
Minnesota	●		●	●		●	●	●		●	
Mississippi	●		●	●		●	●			●	
Missouri	●		●	●		●	●	●	●	●	
Montana	●				●		●				
Nebraska	●		●	●		●	●			●	
Nevada	●				●						
New Hampshire	●		●	●		●			●	●	
New Jersey	●		●	●		●	●	●			
New Mexico	●			●		●					
New York	●		●	●		●	●				
North Carolina	●		●	●		●	●		●		●
United States (Cont'd)											
North Dakota	●		●	●		●					
Ohio	●		●	●			●				
Oklahoma	●		●	●		●			●		
Oregon	●			●	●						
Pennsylvania	●		●	●		●					
Rhode Island	●		●	●		●	●		●	●	
South Carolina	●		●	●		●	●	●	●	●	
South Dakota	●			●	●				●		
Tennessee	●		●			●	●	●	●	●	●
Texas	●		●	●	●		●			●	
Utah	●				●						
Vermont	●		●	●		●	●				
Virginia	●		●	●		●	●	●	●		
Washington	●		●	●		●			●		
West Virginia	●		●	●		●	●		●		
Wisconsin	●		●	●		●	●			●	
Wyoming	●		●	●	●						
Total (United States)	49	0	42	44	12	37	33	6	16	22	4
Canada											
Alberta	●		●	●							
British Columbia	●		●	●	●					●	●
Manitoba	●			●			●			●	
New Brunswick	●		●	●			●		●		
Newfoundland											
Northwest Territories											
Nova Scotia	●		●	●		●	●				
Ontario	●		●	●			●		●		
Prince Edward Island	●		●	●		●				●	
Quebec	●		●	●	●						
Saskatchewan	●			●							
Yukon Territory											
Total (Canada)	9	0	6	8	4	4	2	0	2	3	1

MARTEN
(*Martes americana*)

DESCRIPTION: Martens range in color from light buff to a reddish brown. Usually, the head is lighter in color than the body. Martens commonly exhibit a light color patch on their throat and chest. The body shape is long and slender, and the short legs have relatively large furred feet with semi-retractible claws. The head is relatively small with pronounced round ears. Sexes are similar in appearance but males usually are 15 to 20 percent larger than females. Males weigh up to 5 pounds (2.3 kg) and reach 2 feet (60 cm) in length. The skull has 38 teeth. There are 8 mammae.

HABITAT: The marten inhabits the boreal coniferous forests of Canada and the U.S. It tends to avoid seral forests such as clearcut or burned out areas. However, it has been observed in mixed mature forests.

FOOD HABITS: Martens are primarily carnivorous. Food items include squirrels, rabbits, mice and other small mammals, small birds and their eggs, reptiles and insects, and occasionally berries and nuts.

BEHAVIOR: Martens essentially are nocturnal, seldom active during the day. They tend to be solitary as adults, only pairing briefly during the mating season.

REPRODUCTION: The breeding season is July and August. The gestation period is long and variable (220-275 days) because implantation is delayed. After implantation the fetuses develop quickly and parturition occurs in approximately 28 days. Litters containing 1 to 4 young are born in March or April. The altricial young weigh about 1 ounce (28 g) at birth. They are blind, deaf, practically naked and completely helpless. The newborns' sparse yellow coats become dark gray after 10 days and dark brown in their third week. The young are weaned at 7 weeks of age. Martens reach adult size at 4 to 5 months of age at which time they disperse and become independent. Most martens reach sexual maturity and breed in their second year, therefore females usually bear their first young during their third year.

POPULATION STATUS: The marten population is generally stable in Canada. Attempts to re-establish martens is historic ranges have been somewhat successful in Canada and the U.S. This species increases slowly in new areas because of the time required to reach sexual maturity, their relatively short life span (6-8 years) and territorial behavior.

UTILIZATION: Martens are taken only by trappers. Pelts are used in full garments, as trim and accessories. Recent North American marten harvests have yielded approximately 150 thousand pelts valued at more than 3 million dollars annually.

REFERENCES

ANONYMOUS. 1978. Report on the Status of Canadian Wildlife Used by the Fur Industry. Dept. of Industry, Trade and Commerce, Ottawa. 66 pp.

_____. 1979. Fur Production, 1977-78. Statistics Canada, Ottawa. 17 pp.

BANFIELD, A.W.F. 1974. The Mammals of Canada. Univ. of Toronto Press. 438 pp.

COWAN, I. McTaggart. and C.J. Guiguet. 1965. The Mammals of British Columbia.

Queens Printer, Victoria, B.C. 414 pp.

NORTHCOTT, T. H. 1977. Marten. Canadian Wildlife Service, Dept. of Fisheries and the Environment, Ottawa. 3 pp.

PETERSON, Randolph L. 1973. The Mammals of Eastern Canada. Oxford Univ. Press. Toronto. 465 pp.

Map 15.   **The Range of the Marten in the United States and Canada.**

Fig. 15 **The Management Status of the Marten in the United States and Canada**

STATES, PROVINCES AND TERRITORIES	Present	Total Protection	Hunting Season	Trapping Season	Year-Round Harvesting	Limited Harvesting	Food Resource	Habitat Management	Population Inventories	Special Regulations	Private Lands Leased
United States											
Alabama											
Alaska	●			●		●					
Arizona											
Arkansas											
California	●	●									
Colorado	●			●		●					
Connecticut											
Delaware											
Florida											
Georgia											
Idaho	●			●		●					
Illinois											
Indiana											
Iowa											
Kansas											
Kentucky											
Louisiana											
Maine	●			●		●			●	●	
Maryland											
Massachusetts											
Michigan	●	●									
Minnesota	●	●									
Mississippi											
Missouri											
Montana	●			●		●				●	
Nebraska											
Nevada	●	●									
New Hampshire	●	●									
New Jersey											
New Mexico	●	●									
New York	●			●		●			●	●	
North Carolina											
United States (Cont'd)											
North Dakota											
Ohio											
Oklahoma											
Oregon	●			●		●					
Pennsylvania											
Rhode Island											
South Carolina											
South Dakota											
Tennessee											
Texas											
Utah	●			●		●					
Vermont											
Virginia											
Washington	●			●		●			●		
West Virginia											
Wisconsin	●	●							●		
Wyoming	●			●		●					
Total (United States)	17	7	0	10	0	10	0	0	4	3	0
Canada											
Alberta	●			●		●			●		
British Columbia	●			●		●				●	
Manitoba	●			●		●			●		
New Brunswick	●			●						●	
Newfoundland	●			●		●					
Northwest Territories	●			●		●					
Nova Scotia	●	●									
Ontario	●			●		●			●		
Prince Edward Island											
Quebec	●			●		●					
Saskatchewan	●			●		●				●	
Yukon Territory	●			●		●				●	●
Total (Canada)	11	1	0	10	0	9	0	0	3	4	1

FISHER
(*Martes pennanti*)

DESCRIPTION: The fisher is a very large member of the weasel family. Although a relatively small animal it has a long slender body, short legs and a long bushy tail. The pelage varies from gray to dark brown to nearly black. The male's fur is noticeably longer and coarser than the female's. Adult males usually are 20 percent larger than females; the male's head is noticeably broader than the female's. The tail, feet and nose are black, in contrast with the head and shoulders which are lighter in color and often grizzled in appearance. Adult males range from 33 to 40 inches (84 to 102 cm) in total length (including the tail) and weigh from 4 to as much as 20 pounds (2-9 kg) in rare cases. The skull has 38 teeth. There are 4 mammae.

HABITAT: Fishers prefer mature coniferous and mixed hardwood-softwood forests. They also inhabit cutover forested areas and old burns. They usually are near permanent water sources and wet areas.

FEEDING HABITS: The fisher's diet consists mainly of small mammals, birds, frogs, fish, carrion, and occasionally fruit and nuts. The fisher is the primary predator of porcupines and one of the few predators capable of killing porcupines and escaping damage from the quills. They also occasionally kill foxes, raccoons and deer (under special deep snow conditions).

BEHAVIOR: Fishers are secretive and solitary except when breeding. They are aggressive hunters that may be active at anytime during all seasons. They are excellent swimmers and extremely swift and agile in trees.

REPRODUCTION: Fishers breed during March-April period. Implantation is delayed. After an approximate 51 week gestation period, 1 to 4 young (usually 3) are born. The female is receptive for breeding soon after parturition, and the male becomes solitary soon after mating. The young are weaned at about 4 months of age. Both males and females are sexually mature at about 12 months of age. Females breed shortly thereafter, but males may not breed until later.

POPULATION STATUS: The historic range of the fisher was drastically reduced by the logging and clearing operations of early settlers, especially in the United States. Reforestation efforts and changes in land-use practices have restored some of the fisher's habitats and historic range. Transplanting programs have reestablished the fisher in several areas, particularly in West Virginia, Maryland, Nova Scotia and Montana. The present North American fisher population appears secure and relatively stable.

UTILIZATION: Fishers are taken primarily by trapping techniques. The fur is valuable, especially the pelt of the female which is less coarse than the male's. In recent years the North American harvest of fishers has yielded 15 to 20 thousand pelts valued at 1.5 to 2 million dollars annually.

REFERENCES

ANONYMOUS. 1978. Report on the Status of Canadian Wildlife Used by the Fur Industry. Dept. of Industry, Trade and Commerce, Ottawa. 66 pp.

_____. 1979. Fur Production, 1977-78. Statistics Canada, Ottawa. 17 pp.

ANTHONY, H.E. 1928. Field Book of North American Mammals. G.P. Putnam's Sons, N.Y., New York. 674 pp.

BANFIELD, A.W.F. 1974. The Mammals of Canada. Univ. of Toronto Press. 438 pp.

BURT, W.H., and R.P. Grossenheider. 1976. A Field Guide to the Mammals. 3rd Edition. Houghton Mifflin Co., Boston. 289 pp.

COULTER, W.M. 1960. The Status and Distribution of Fisher in Maine. Jour. of Mamm. 41: 1-9.

COWAN, I. McTaggart. and C.J. Guiguet. 1965. The Mammals of British Columbia. Queens Printer, Victoria, B.C. 414 pp.

DANIEL, M.J. 1960. Porcupine Quills in Viscera of Fisher. J. of Mammal. 41: 133.

DEEMS, E.F., and D. Pursley. 1978. North American Furbearers, Their Management, Research and Harvest Status in 1976. International Association of Fish and Wildlife Agencies. 171 pp.

GODIN, A.J. 1977. Wild Mammals of New England. Johns Hopkins Press, Baltimore, Maryland. 304 pp.

HALL, E.R., and K.R. Kelson. 1959. Mammals of North America. Ronald Press Co., N.Y., New York. 1083 pp.

HAMILTON, W.J., and A.H. Cook. 1955. The Biology and Management of the Fisher in New York. N.Y. Fish and Game J. 2: 13-35.

KELLY, G.M. 1977. Fisher (*Martes pennanti*). Biology in the White Mountain National Forest and Adjacent Areas. Ph.D Thesis, Univ. of Mass., Amherst. 178 pp.

WALKER, E.P. 1975. Mammals of the World (third ed.). Johns Hopkins Press, Baltimore, Maryland. 1500 pp.

WECKWERTH, R.P., and P.L. Wright. 1968. Results of Transplanting Fishers in Montana. J. Wildl. Manage. 32: 977-980.

Map 16.

The Range of the Fisher in the United States
and Canada.

Fig. 16

The Management Status of the Fisher in the United States and Canada

STATES, PROVINCES AND TERRITORIES	Present	Total Protection	Hunting Season	Trapping Season	Year-Round Harvesting	Limited Harvesting	Food Resource	Habitat Management	Population Inventories	Special Regulations	Private Lands Leased
United States											
Alabama											
Alaska											
Arizona											
Arkansas											
California	●	●									
Colorado											
Connecticut											
Delaware											
Florida											
Georgia											
Idaho	●	●									
Illinois											
Indiana											
Iowa											
Kansas											
Kentucky											
Louisiana											
Maine	●			●		●			●	●	
Maryland	●			●		●				●	
Massachusetts	●			●		●				●	
Michigan	●	●									
Minnesota	●			●		●			●	●	
Mississippi											
Missouri											
Montana	●	●								●	
Nebraska											
Nevada											
New Hampshire	●		●	●		●			●	●	
New Jersey											
New Mexico											
New York	●			●		●			●		
North Carolina											

STATES, PROVINCES AND TERRITORIES	Present	Total Protection	Hunting Season	Trapping Season	Year-Round Harvesting	Limited Harvesting	Food Resource	Habitat Management	Population Inventories	Special Regulations	Private Lands Leased
United States (Cont'd)											
North Dakota	●	●									
Ohio											
Oklahoma											
Oregon	●	●									
Pennsylvania											
Rhode Island	●	●									
South Carolina											
South Dakota											
Tennessee											
Texas											
Utah											
Vermont	●			●		●			●		
Virginia											
Washington	●	●									
West Virginia	●			●		●			●		
Wisconsin	●	●							●	●	
Wyoming	●	●									
Total (United States)	18	10	1	8	0	8	0	0	7	7	0
Canada											
Alberta	●			●		●				●	
British Columbia	●			●		●					●
Manitoba	●			●		●				●	
New Brunswick	●			●					●		
Newfoundland											
Northwest Territories	●			●		●					
Nova Scotia	●		●	●		●				●	
Ontario	●			●		●			●		
Prince Edward Island											
Quebec	●			●		●					
Saskatchewan	●			●		●				●	
Yukon Territory	●			●		●				●	
Total (Canada)	10	0	1	10	0	9	0	0	2	5	1

Short-tailed weasel in winter coat.

SHORT-TAILED WEASEL
(*Mustela erminea*)

DESCRIPTION: The short-tailed weasel is an alert, active, relatively small, short-legged, slender-bodied carnivore with a black-tipped tail. The eyes are small, beady and black with no discernible pupil. The ears are wide-set, small and rounded. Each foot has 5 toes with short, nonretractible claws. The pelage color varies with the seasons. In summer, the face, head and neck, back, sides and tail are light brown, while the chin, throat and belly are whitish in color. In winter, in northern latitudes and high elevations, the entire pelt is white except the permanently black-tipped tail. Annual color changes (molts) involve periods of mottled black and brown coats during the fall and spring. The guard hairs and underfur are relatively short and dense. The sexes are similar in appearance but males are much larger than females. Adult males weigh 2.5 to 6.8 ounces (71-193 g) and attain lengths of 8 to 13 inches (20-33 cm) while the females weigh 1 to 3 ounces (28-85 g) and attain lengths of 7 to 11 inches (18-28 cm). The tail comprises 30 to 45 percent of the total length. The skull has 34 teeth. There are 8 to 10 mammae.

HABITAT: Short-tailed weasels prefer coniferous woodlands associated with open fields, brushlands and abundant sources of fresh water. The absence of suitable drinking water appears to be a limiting factor even when prey and den sites are abundant. Short-tailed weasels den in hollow roots and trees, underground burrows and similar cavities in undisturbed areas.

FEEDING HABITS: The short-tailed weasel's diet consists mainly of mice and other small mammals although it will eat almost any fresh meat. It kills prey by biting the neck at the base of the skull and is capable of killing animals larger than itself. The short-tailed weasel is so dependent upon mice and small mammals that its population size and distribution vary in response to changes in those prey species.

BEHAVIOR: Short-tailed weasels usually are nocturnal but frequently are active in the daytime. Weasels appear to hunt certain coverts regularly but often do not forage in the same specific area on two consecutive nights. Excess food is cached for later use. This weasel is an excellent tree climber. Short-tailed weasels travel up to 3 miles (4.8 km) in a single foray. They investigate every single hole, burrow and crevice they encounter. Weasels can squeeze through any hole the size of their head or larger. Like other weasels, the short-tailed weasel's anal glands secrete a strong acrid musk.

REPRODUCTION: Adults pair throughout much of the year. Mating occurs during midsummer, implantation is delayed and the gestation period is 8½ to 10 months. Litters contain 4 to 8 (6 is average) altricial young. The newborn are blind for about 35 days, but are weaned by about 6 weeks of age and are full grown by the end of their first summer. Short-tailed weasels are sexually mature at approximately one year of age.

POPULATION STATUS: The North American short-tailed weasel population is relatively stable and directly related to the amount and quality of habitat. Good habitats support as many as 20 or more short-tailed weasels per square mile (2.6 km²) when prey is abundant.

UTILIZATION: Historically, white weasel pelts (ermine) were in great demand for royal adornments. Short-tailed weasel pelts comprise the vast majority of "ermine skins" from

North America. In recent years the market value of weasel pelts has been relatively low and stable considering inflation. North American harvests of short-tailed and long-tailed weasels are rarely segregated therefore annual pelt harvest records include both species. The recent annual harvests of North American weasels (short-tailed and long-tailed) range from about 80,000 to 125,000 pelts with total values of $115,000 to $125,000.

REFERENCES

ANONYMOUS. 1978. Report on the Status of Canadian Wildlife Used by the Fur Industry. Revised Edition (1977). Dept. of Industry, Trade and Commerce, Ottawa, Canada, in association with the Canada Fur Council.

BANFIELD, A.W.F. 1974. The Mammals of Canada. Univ. of Toronto Press. 438 pp.

BURT, W.H., and R.P. Grossenheider. 1976. A Field Guide to the Mammals. 3rd Edition. Houghton Mifflin Co., Boston. 289 pp.

DEEMS, E.F., and D. Pursley. 1978. North American Furbearers, Their Management, Research and Harvest Status in 1976. International Association of Fish and Wildlife Agencies. 171 pp.

GLOVER, F.A. 1943B. A Study of the Winter Activities of the New York Weasel. Penn. Game News. 14(6): 8-9.

HALL, E.R. 1951. American Weasels. Univ. Kansas, Museum of Nat. Hist. Vol. 4. 1-466 pp.

_____, and K.R. Kelson. 1959. Mammals of North America. Ronald Press Co., New York. 1083 pp.

HAMILTON, W.J. 1933. The Weasels of New York. American Midland Nat. 14: 289-344.

PETERSON, Randolph L. 1966. The Mammals of Eastern Canada. Toronto, Oxford University Press.

QUICK, H.F. 1944. Habits and Economics of the New York Weasel in Michigan. Jour. Wildl. Manage. 8: 76-78.

SETON, E.T. 1929. Lives of Game Animals. Doubleday Doran and Co., New York, N.Y. Vol. 2. 598-599 pp.

TECHLEITNER, R.R. 1969. Wild Mammals of Colorado. Pruett Pub. Co., Boulder, Colorado.

WALKER, E.P. 1975. Mammals of the World (third ed.). Johns Hopkins Press, Baltimore, Maryland. 1500 pp.

Map 17. The Range of the Short-Tailed Weasel in the United States and Canada.

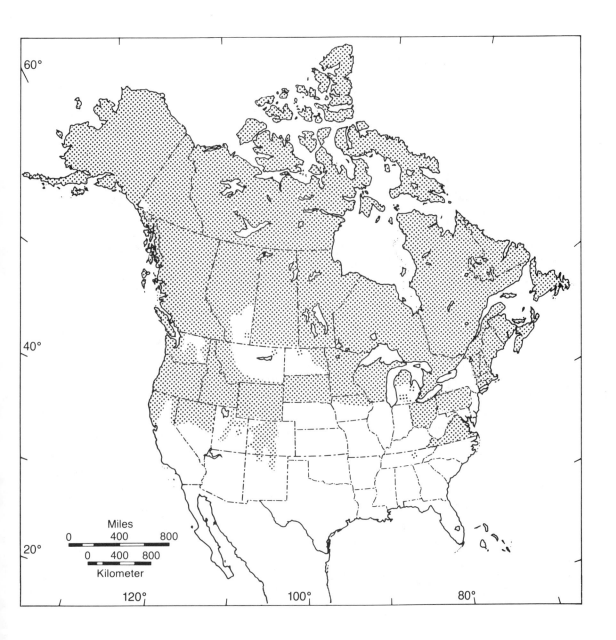

Miles
0   400   800

0   400   800
Kilometer

137

Fig. 17

The Management Status of the Short-Tailed Weasel in the United States and Canada

STATES, PROVINCES AND TERRITORIES	Present	Total Protection	Hunting Season	Trapping Season	Year-Round Harvesting	Limited Harvesting	Food Resource	Habitat Management	Population Inventories	Special Regulations	Private Lands Leased
United States											
Alabama											
Alaska	●			●	●						
Arizona											
Arkansas											
California	●			●	●						
Colorado	●			●		●					
Connecticut	●		●	●		●				●	
Delaware	●				●						
Florida											
Georgia											
Idaho	●		●	●	●						
Illinois											
Indiana											
Iowa	●			●		●			●	●	
Kansas											
Kentucky											
Louisiana											
Maine	●			●		●					
Maryland											
Massachusetts	●		●	●	●						
Michigan	●				●						
Minnesota	●				●					●	
Mississippi											
Missouri											
Montana	●				●						
Nebraska											
Nevada	●				●						
New Hampshire	●				●					●	
New Jersey											
New Mexico	●			●		●					
New York	●		●	●	●						
North Carolina											
United States (Cont'd)											
North Dakota	●			●	●						
Ohio	●			●							
Oklahoma											
Oregon	●			●	●						
Pennsylvania	●		●	●	●						
Rhode Island	●		●	●	●				●	●	
South Carolina											
South Dakota	●			●	●						
Tennessee	●		●	●	●						
Texas											
Utah	●				●						
Vermont	●			●	●						
Virginia	●			●							
Washington	●			●	●				●		
West Virginia											
Wisconsin	●			●	●						
Wyoming	●		●	●	●						
Total (United States)	29	0	8	21	17	11	0	0	4	4	0
Canada											
Alberta	●			●		●				●	
British Columbia	●			●		●					●
Manitoba	●			●		●				●	
New Brunswick	●			●					●		
Newfoundland	●			●		●					
Northwest Territories	●			●		●					
Nova Scotia	●		●	●							
Ontario	●			●		●			●		
Prince Edward Island	●			●		●				●	
Quebec	●			●		●					
Saskatchewan	●			●		●				●	
Yukon Territory	●			●		●				●	
Total (Canada)	12	0	1	12	0	10	0	0	2	5	1

Long-tailed weasel.

Long-tailed weasel in winter coat.

LONG-TAILED WEASEL
(*Mustela frenata*)

DESCRIPTION: The long-tailed weasel is very similar in appearance to the short-tailed weasel except the former is larger and its tail is significantly longer. In some southern areas the long-tailed weasel exhibits white or yellowish facial markings (bridles). The sexes are similar in appearance except males are larger than females. Adult males weigh 6½ to 12½ ounces (184-354 g) and reach lengths of 13 to 22 inches (33-56 cm) while adult females weigh from 2½ to 7 ounces (71-198 g) and attain lengths of 11 to 15 inches (28-38 cm). The tail comprises about 44 percent of the total length. The skull has 34 teeth. There are 8 mammae.

HABITAT: Long-tailed weasels occupy a wide variety of habitats. They inhabit both coniferous and deciduous forest edges, brushlands, marshes and agricultural areas, where prey species, den sites and fresh water sources are available. Den sites include animal burrows, hollow trees, logs, stumps as well as cavities in and under buildings and haystacks. A typical den has 2 surface openings located about 2 feet (0.6 m) apart which are connected by a burrow that is 3 to 10 feet (0.9-3 m) long.

FEEDING HABITS: Like the short-tailed weasel, the long-tailed weasel preys primarily on mice and other small mammals, but, unlike short-tailed weasels, the long-tailed weasel is not entirely dependent on small mammals for food. When mice and similar sized mammals are scarce, long-tailed weasels pursue gophers, rabbits, birds (including domestic poultry) and even reptiles and insects. Long-tailed weasels will attack animals that are much larger than themselves. In northern areas, under thick snow cover conditions, the males typically feed on larger prey above the snow while females prey on small mammals under the snow. Adults usually consume an amount of food equal to ⅓ their weight every 24 hours. Young growing weasels consume proportionately more food than adults in every 24 hour period.

BEHAVIOR: Like the short-tailed weasel, long-tailed weasels are primarily nocturnal, they cache excess food and are excellent tree climbers even though they seldom hunt in trees. Long-tailed weasels tend to travel farther than short-tailed weasels and may travel 4 miles or more on a single foray. Long-tailed weasels in open timber appear to travel farther than those in dense woodlands and brushlands. The anal glands and musk are similar to those of the mink and other weasels.

REPRODUCTION: Long-tailed weasels mate in late summer (July-September). Females are induced ovulators and remain in heat for several weeks if not bred early. There is a long delay in implantation and parturition usually occurs about 280 days after impregnation. Litters contain from 1 to 9 altricial young. The newborn open their eyes at 5 weeks of age and begin to grow and mature rapidly. Females become sexually mature at 3 months of age and breed during their first summer but males do not breed until their second summer.

POPULATION STATUS: The North American long-tailed weasel population is relatively widespread, stable and apparently directly related to habitat conditions. This weasel is apparently more adaptable than the short-tailed weasel and occurs in a wide variety of habitats. Population densities vary from one long-tailed weasel per 6 acres (2.4

ha) in chestnut oak habitats to one per 13 acres (5.3 ha) in open forests. Some researchers feel that reductions in sources of drinking water and the absence of grain sheaves and haystacks in today's farmlands have somewhat reduced long-tailed weasel densities by reducing den sites and prey availability in many areas.

UTILIZATION: The long-tailed weasel does not exhibit a white (ermine) winter coat in the southern portion of its range and most brown weasel pelts marketed in North America come from this species. In northern portions of its distribution, long-tails do have a white pelt and annually are worth two to three times the value of short-tailed weasels. See the utilization section in the short-tailed weasel for harvest and economic information.

REFERENCES

ANONYMOUS. 1978. Report on the Status of Canadian Wildlife Used by the Fur Industry. Revised Edition (1977). Dept. of Industry, Trade and Commerce, Ottawa, Canada, in association with the Canada Fur Council.

BANFIELD, A.W.F. 1974. The Mammals of Canada. Univ. of Toronto Press. 438 pp.

BURT, W.H., and R.P. Grossenheider. 1964. A Field Guide to the Mammals. Houghton Mifflin Co., Boston. 289 pp.

DEEMS, E.F., and D. Pursley. 1978. North American Furbearers, Their Management, Research and Harvest Status in 1976. International Association of Fish and Wildlife Agencies. 171 pp.

GLOVER, F.A. 1943b. A Study of the Winter Activities of the New York Weasel. Penn. Game News. 14(6): 8-9.

HALL, E.R. 1951. American Weasels. Univ. Kansas, Museum of Nat. Hist. Vol. 4. 446 pp.

_____, and K.R. Kelson. 1959. Mammals of North America. Ronald Press Co., New York. 1083 pp.

HAMILTON, W.J. 1933. The Weasels of New York. American Midland Nat. 14: 289-344.

QUICK, H.F. 1944. Habits and Economics of the New York Weasel in Michigan. Jour. Wildl. Manage. 8: 76-78.

SETON, E.T. 1929. Lives of Game Animals. Doubleday Doran and Co., New York, N.Y. Vol. 2. 598-599 pp.

TECHLEITNER, R.R. 1969. Wild Mammals of Colorado. Pruett Pub. Co., Boulder, Colorado. 254 pp.

WALKER, E.P. 1975. Mammals of the World (third ed.). Johns Hopkins Press, Baltimore, Maryland. 1500 pp.

Map 18. The Range of the Long-Tailed Weasel in the United States and Canada.

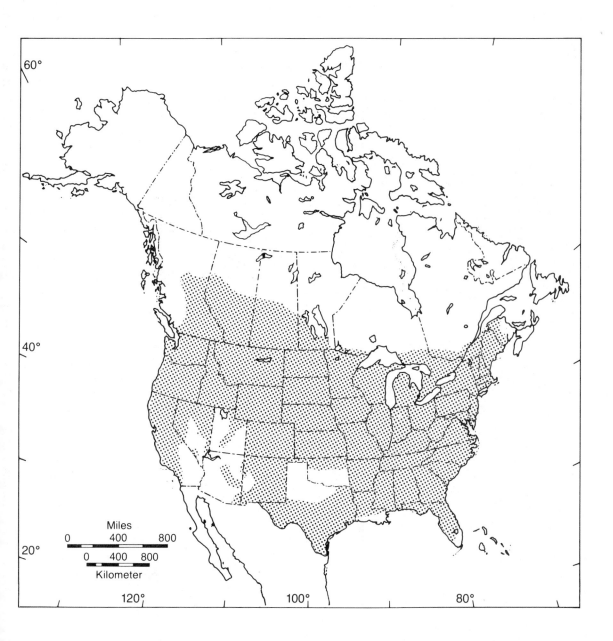

Fig. 18

The Management Status of the Long-Tailed Weasel in the United States and Canada

STATES, PROVINCES AND TERRITORIES	Present	Total Protection	Hunting Season	Trapping Season	Year-Round Harvesting	Limited Harvesting	Food Resource	Habitat Management	Population Inventories	Special Regulations	Private Lands Leased
United States											
Alabama	●		●		●					●	
Alaska											
Arizona	●		●	●		●				●	
Arkansas	●		●	●		●					
California	●			●	●						
Colorado	●			●		●					
Connecticut	●		●	●		●				●	
Delaware	●					●					
Florida	●	●								●	
Georgia	●			●		●				●	
Idaho	●		●	●	●						
Illinois	●			●		●			●	●	
Indiana	●		●	●		●			●		
Iowa	●			●		●			●	●	
Kansas	●			●		●					
Kentucky	●			●		●					
Louisiana	●	●									
Maine	●			●		●					
Maryland	●			●		●					
Massachusetts	●		●	●	●						
Michigan	●				●						
Minnesota	●				●					●	
Mississippi	●			●		●				●	
Missouri	●		●	●	●				●	●	
Montana	●				●						
Nebraska	●				●						
Nevada	●				●						
New Hampshire	●				●				●		
New Jersey	●			●		●			●		
New Mexico	●			●		●					
New York	●		●	●	●						
North Carolina	●			●		●					
United States (Cont'd)											
North Dakota	●			●		●					
Ohio	●			●							
Oklahoma	●		●	●		●					
Oregon	●			●	●						
Pennsylvania	●		●	●	●						
Rhode Island	●	○		●	●				●	●	
South Carolina	●			●		●				●	
South Dakota	●			●		●					
Tennessee	●		●	●		●					
Texas	●				●						
Utah	●				●						
Vermont	●			●		●					
Virginia	●			●	●						
Washington	●			●		●			●		
West Virginia	●			●	●						
Wisconsin	●			●	●						
Wyoming	●		●	●	●						
Total (United States)	48	2	13	37	21	24	0	0	8	12	0
Canada											
Alberta	●			●		●				●	
British Columbia	●			●		●					●
Manitoba	●			●		●				●	
New Brunswick	●			●					●		
Newfoundland											
Northwest Territories											
Nova Scotia											
Ontario	●			●					●		
Prince Edward Island											
Quebec	●			●		●					
Saskatchewan	●			●		●				●	
Yukon Territory											
Total (Canada)	7	0	0	7	0	5	0	0	2	3	1

MINK
(*Mustela vison*)

DESCRIPTION: Mink have long thin bodies and necks, small ears, short legs and bushy tails that comprise about 1/3 of the total length. The pelage is soft, thick and chestnut-brown to black with white spots occurring on the throat, chest, chin and anal regions. Adult males sometimes weigh over 3 pounds (1.6 kg) and attain lengths of nearly 28 inches (70 cm). Females are noticeably smaller than males. The skull has 34 teeth. There are 8 mammae.

HABITAT: Mink inhabit every North American province and state except Arizona. They generally occur in or near some type of wetland habitat — marshes, swamps, lakes, rivers, streams, canals, ponds and ditches. However they may travel considerable distances from wetlands when hunting. The availability of adequate den sites (undisturbed by other animals and man) appears to be a limiting factor to mink populations in some areas.

FEEDING HABITS: The mink's diet is characterized by a diversity of prey items because the mink forages in both aquatic and terrestrial environments. Mink feed on rabbits, muskrats and other small mammals, birds, fish, reptiles, amphibians, crustaceans and insects. The extent of prey utilization appears to be directly related to prey abundance and availability. Mink are occasionally cannibalistic.

BEHAVIOR: Mink are primarily nocturnal although occasionally active during the day. Male mink spend nearly 90 percent of their activity periods in pursuit of prey. Females become less active during gestation and more active after parturition. Mink are excellent swimmers and capable tree climbers.

REPRODUCTION: Mink are promiscuous. The breeding season is late February to early April (primarily March). Males are more active and apparently more aggressive during the mating season. Implantation is delayed and the gestation period varies from 40 to 75 days (average 51 days). The young are born 28 to 30 days after implantation. Litters contain 1 to 8 young (average is 4). The altricial young are raised solely by the mother. The female and her young constitute a family unit until the fall when the young disperse and become independent.

POPULATION STATUS: Mink generally are abundant throughout their range in North America. Local population fluctuations occur but wetland preservation and water quality enhancement programs are tending to conserve and preserve much of the mink's primary habitats.

UTILIZATION: Mink pelts are used in full length garments, trimmings and accessories. The baccula are used in jewelry. Most of North America's mink fur production comes from mink ranches. In recent years the annual harvests of ranched minks have exceeded 4 million pelts. Recent North American wild mink harvests have yielded 300 to 400 thousand pelts valued at more than 5 million dollars annually.

REFERENCES

ANONYMOUS. 1978. Report on the Status of Canadian Wildlife Used by the Fur

Industry. Dept. of Industry, Trade and Commerce, Ottawa. 66 pp.

_____. 1979. Fur Production, 1977-78. Statistics Canada, Ottawa. 17 pp.

BANFIELD, A.W.F. 1974. The Mammals of Canada. Univ. of Toronto Press. 438 pp.

BURT, W.H., and R.P. Grossenheider. 1964. A Field Guide to the Mammals. Houghton Mifflin Co., Boston. 289 pp.

CHAPMAN, J.A., and G.A. Feldhamer. 1982. Wild Mammals of North America. The North American Mink. 1,000 pp.

COWAN, I. McTaggart, and C.J. Guiguet. 1965. The Mammals of British Columbia. Queens Printer, Victoria, B.C. 414 pp.

DEEMS, E.F., and D. Pursley. 1978. North American Furbearers, Their Management, Research and Harvest Status in 1976. International Association of Fish and Wildlife Agencies. 171 pp.

ENDERS, R.K. 1952. Reproduction in the Mink. Proc. Am. Phil. Soc. 96: 691-755.

ERLINGE, S. 1972. Interspecific Relations between Otter (*Lutra lutra*) and Mink (*Mustela vison*) in Sweden. Oikos. 23: 327-335.

GERRELL, R. 1969. Activity Patterns of the Mink (*Mustela vison*) Schreber in Southern Sweden. Oikos 20: 451-460.

_____. 1970. Home Ranges and Movements of the Mink in Southern Sweden. Oikos. 21: 160-173.

HANSSON, A. 1947. The Physiology of Reproduction in Mink (*Mustela vison*) Schreber with Special Reference to Delayed Implantation. Acta. Zool. 28: 1-136.

JACKSON, H.H.T. 1961. Mammals of Wisconsin. Univ. Wisconsin Press, Madison. xiii + 504 pp.

LOWERY, G.H. 1974. The Mammals of Louisiana and its Adjacent Waters. The Louisiana State Univ. Press, Baton Rouge. 565 pp.

MARSHALL, W.H. 1936. A Study of the Winter Activity of the Mink. J. of Mammal. 17: 382-392.

PALMISANO, A.W. 1971. Louisiana's Fur Industry. Commercial Wildlife Work Unit Report of Louisiana Wildlife and Fisheries Commission to U.S. Army Corps of Engineers. New Orleans District. Mimeographed.

PETERSON, Randolph L. 1973. The Mammals of Eastern Canada. Oxford Univ. Press. Toronto. 464 pp.

PRENTICE, A.C. 1976. A Candid View of the Fur Industry. Clay Publishing Co. Ltd., Bewdley, Ontario. 319 pp.

ST. AMANT, L.S. 1959. Louisiana Wildlife Inventory and Management Plan. Louisiana Wildlife and Fisheries Commission. xx + 329 pp.

Map 19. The Range of the Mink in the United States and Canada.

Fig. 19 The Management Status of the Mink in the United States and Canada

STATES, PROVINCES AND TERRITORIES	Present	Total Protection	Hunting Season	Trapping Season	Year-Round Harvesting	Limited Harvesting	Food Resource	Habitat Management	Population Inventories	Special Regulations	Private Lands Leased
United States											
Alabama	●			●		●				●	
Alaska	●			●		●					
Arizona											
Arkansas	●		●	●		●					
California	●			●		●					
Colorado	●			●		●					
Connecticut	●			●		●		●		●	
Delaware	●			●							
Florida	●		●	●		●			●	●	
Georgia	●			●		●				●	
Idaho	●			●		●					
Illinois	●			●		●			●	●	
Indiana	●		●	●		●		●	●		
Iowa	●			●		●			●	●	
Kansas	●			●		●					
Kentucky	●		●	●		●					
Louisiana	●			●		●					●
Maine	●			●		●					
Maryland	●			●		●				●	●
Massachusetts	●			●		●					
Michigan	●		●	●		●					
Minnesota	●			●		●		●	●		
Mississippi	●			●		●				●	
Missouri	●			●		●			●	●	
Montana	●			●		●				●	●
Nebraska	●			●		●				●	
Nevada	●			●		●			●		
New Hampshire	●			●		●				●	●
New Jersey	●			●		●			●		
New Mexico	●	●									
New York	●			●		●				●	●
North Carolina	●			●		●					●

STATES, PROVINCES AND TERRITORIES	Present	Total Protection	Hunting Season	Trapping Season	Year-Round Harvesting	Limited Harvesting	Food Resource	Habitat Management	Population Inventories	Special Regulations	Private Lands Leased
United States (Cont'd)											
North Dakota	●			●		●			●		●
Ohio	●		●	●							
Oklahoma	●		●	●		●					
Oregon	●			●		●					
Pennsylvania	●			●		●					
Rhode Island	●			●		●			●	●	
South Carolina	●		●	●		●				●	
South Dakota	●			●		●					
Tennessee	●		●	●		●		●			●
Texas	●		●	●	●					●	
Utah	●			●		●					
Vermont	●			●		●					
Virginia	●			●		●					
Washington	●			●		●			●		
West Virginia	●			●		●					
Wisconsin	●			●		●		●		●	●
Wyoming	●			●		●					
Total (United States)	48	1	10	47	1	44	0	5	11	18	8
Canada											
Alberta	●			●		●				●	
British Columbia	●			●		●					●
Manitoba	●			●		●				●	
New Brunswick	●			●					●		
Newfoundland	●			●		●					
Northwest Territories	●			●		●					
Nova Scotia	●		●	●							
Ontario	●			●		●			●		
Prince Edward Island	●			●		●				●	
Quebec	●			●		●					
Saskatchewan	●			●		●				●	
Yukon Territory	●			●		●				●	
Total (Canada)	12	0	1	12	0	10	0	0	2	5	1

150

WOLVERINE
(*Gulo gulo*)

DESCRIPTION: The wolverine resembles a small bear. It is distinguished by an arched back, short bushy tail, relatively long legs, and large feet. The pelage is long, usually dark brown (lighter on the head) with light-colored stripes extending from the shoulders, along the sides, joining on the rump and base of the tail. The head is broad, tapering to a prominent black muzzle. The ears are wide-set, relatively small and rounded. Each foot has 5 toes with relatively long, non-retractable claws. Sexes are similar in appearance except males are larger than females. Adults attain total lengths of 36 to 41 inches (91 - 104 cm) including the 7 to 9 inch (18 - 23 cm) tail and weigh 35 to 60 pounds (16 - 27 kg). The skull has 38 teeth. There are 4 mammae.

HABITAT: Historically, wolverines inhabited most of the boreal forests in North America. In recent times the wolverine range's southern boundaries have moved northward and today it is most common in Alaska and Canada in areas between the timberline and the arctic coast. In the conterminious U.S. wolverines inhabit the higher ranges of the Rocky Mountains in Idaho, Montana, Wyoming, Colorado and possibly Utah. They also occur in the higher elevations of the Cascade Mountains in Washington and Oregon, in the Sierra Mountains and upper Coast Range in California.

FEEDING HABITS: Wolverines are omnivores. Their diet includes a wide variety of plant material, including fruits, berries, nuts and roots, as well as animals, including small mammals, birds, fish and carrion. Wolverines are known to attack larger ungulates such as deer, goats, sheep and caribou.

BEHAVIOR: Wolverines primarily are solitary and may be active at any hour of the day or night. They are extremely powerful and aggressive animals for their size. Their feats of strength are legendary among trappers who view the wolverine as a furbearer, trap robber, and cabin plunderer. Wolverines are extremely territorial and therefore do not occur in high densities in any habitat type or area.

REPRODUCTION: The breeding season is late April to September. Implantation is delayed and gestation is extremely variable. Implantation usually occurs in January or February and parturition occurs about 60 days later. Litter sizes range from 1 to 5 (average is 2 or 3) and the altricial newborn have fuzzy, creamy-white coats. Dens are located in sheltered areas in rocky out-crops, under logs or tree roots. The young are weaned at about 8 or 9 weeks of age and remain with the mother through their first winter but disperse the following spring. Females are sexually mature and capable of breeding in their second year. Males may not breed until later.

POPULATION STATUS: North America's wolverine population is generally stable with the exception of eastern Canada where habitat loss is a significant factor. Even though pelt prices have increased progressively and substantially during the last decade, the harvest has remained relatively constant.

UTILIZATION: Wolverine pelts are prized as parka trim and sub-zero clothing because of their warmth and ability to remain frost free. Wolverines are taken primarily by trappers, but in some northern areas they are hunted as trophy game animals. In recent years, the annual North American (Alaska and Canada) harvest of wolverines has remained relatively stable at about 2,000 pelts, and the total annual harvest values range between $250,000 and $300,000.

REFERENCES

ANONYMOUS. 1978. Report on the Status of Canadian Wildlife Used by the Fur Industry. Department of Industry, Trade and Commerce, Ottawa in Association with the Canada Fur Council. 66 pp.

_____. 1979. Fur Production, 1977-78. Statistics Canada, Ottawa. 17 pp.

BANFIELD. A.W.F. 1974. The Mammals of Canada. Univ. of Toronto Press. 438 pp.

BURT, W.H., and R. P. Grossenheider. 1964. A Field Guide to the Mammals. Houghton Mifflin Co., Boston. 289 pp.

COWAN, I. McTaggart, and C. J. Guiguet, 1965. The Mammals of British Columbia. Queens Printer, Victoria, B.C. 414 pp.

DEEMS, E. F., and D. Pursley. 1978. North American Furbearers, Their Management, Research and Harvest Status in 1976. International Association of Fish and Wildlife Agencies. 171 pp.

PETERSON, Randolph L. 1973. The Mammals of Eastern Canada. Oxford, Unvi. Press, Toronto. 465 pp.

154

Map 20.   The Range of the Wolverine in the United States
and Canada.

Fig. 20

The Management Status of the Wolverine in the United States and Canada

STATES, PROVINCES AND TERRITORIES	Present	Total Protection	Hunting Season	Trapping Season	Year-Round Harvesting	Limited Harvesting	Food Resource	Habitat Management	Population Inventories	Special Regulations	Private Lands Leased
United States											
Alabama											
Alaska	●		●	●		●			●		
Arizona											
Arkansas											
California	●	●									
Colorado	●	●									
Connecticut											
Delaware											
Florida											
Georgia											
Idaho	●	●									
Illinois											
Indiana											
Iowa											
Kansas											
Kentucky											
Louisiana											
Maine											
Maryland											
Massachusetts											
Michigan											
Minnesota		●									
Mississippi											
Missouri											
Montana	●			●		●			●	●	
Nebraska											
Nevada											
New Hampshire											
New Jersey											
New Mexico											
New York											
North Carolina											
United States (Cont'd)											
North Dakota											
Ohio											
Oklahoma											
Oregon	●	●									
Pennsylvania											
Rhode Island											
South Carolina											
South Dakota											
Tennessee											
Texas											
Utah		●									
Vermont											
Virginia											
Washington	●	●									
West Virginia											
Wisconsin											
Wyoming	●	●									
Total (United States)	8	8	1	2	0	2	0	0	2	1	0
Canada											
Alberta	●		●	●						●	
British Columbia	●		●	●		●					●
Manitoba	●			●		●				●	
New Brunswick											
Newfoundland	●	●									
Northwest Territories	●			●		●					
Nova Scotia											
Ontario	●			●		●			●		
Prince Edward Island											
Quebec	●			●		●					
Saskatchewan	●			●	●						
Yukon Territory	●		●	●		●				●	
Total (Canada)	9	1	3	8	1	6	0	0	1	3	1

BADGER
(*Taxidea taxus*)

DESCRIPTION: The badger is a thickset, medium-sized mammal with a broad head, short thick neck (the same width as the head) and a short bushy tail. Its ears are rounded and set low on its head. The fur is short on the back and longer on the sides, giving the badger its characteristic squat appearance. The skin is loose and tough. The general coloration is gray with a slight yellowish cast. The brownish face is marked with a white stripe which runs from the nose to the crown of the head and sometimes onto the neck and back. The feet and backs of the ears are black. There are five toes on each foot and the claws on the front feet are exceptionally long. The sexes are colored alike and show no marked seasonal changes. Adults average 26 to 35 inches (66 - 89 cm) in length and 13 to 30 pounds (5.9 - 13 kg) in weight. The skull has 34 teeth. There are 8 mammae.

HABITAT: Badgers prefer open country (prairies and plains) where ground squirrels, gophers and other burrowing mammals are abundant. They dig shallow burrows about 12 inches (30 cm) in diameter while searching for prey. Some badgers live in open woodlands but most prefer the prairie-type habitats.

FEEDING HABITS: Badgers are strictly carnivorous. Rodents and rabbits are their primary food items. Badgers also eat moles, reptiles, turtle eggs, ground nesting birds and their eggs, scorpions, insects, snails and fish when available. Badgers eat carrion occasionally and rarely store their food.

BEHAVIOR: Badgers usually spend their lives within a home range of 1 to 2 square miles (2.6 - 5.1 km²) as long as food is plentiful. They are mostly nocturnal but occasionally forage in the early morning or late evening. In the northern portion of their range, badgers store a large amount of body fat during the late summer and fall which allows them to hibernate during extreme winter weather periods. In the southern part of their range they are active throughout the winter. Badgers are vigorous diggers and their tunneling activities provide them with food as well as protection from surface dwelling predators. Coyotes and avian predators apparently follow hunting badgers to catch those rodents that escape while the badger is digging. The badger is a formidable adversary when cornered. Its thick fur, loose and tough skin, large claws, sharp teeth and strength are difficult to overcome. Badgers hiss, grunt, growl and snarl when cornered or fighting. The badger has two pairs of scent glands — one pair on the belly and the other near the anus. The anal glands secrete a strong but relatively inoffensive odor. To release this scent, the badger must raise its tail but it cannot direct the spray accurately as do its relatives, the skunks. Adults generally lead solitary lives.

REPRODUCTION: During the breeding season (August-September), a deep burrow and an enlarged chamber are dug about 2 to 3 feet (0.5 - 1.0m) below of the surface of the ground. Delayed implantation follows fertilization in badgers and the entire gestation period varies from 6 to 9 months in length. Parturition occurs in the March-June period. Litters contain 1 to 7 altricial young (averge is 3). The young open their eyes at about 5 weeks of age and are weaned when half-grown. Over half of the females breed during their first year.

POPULATION STATUS: Intensive land development and agriculture activities have restricted historic badger habitats. However, timber removal operations have created new badger habitats and the overall North American population of badgers appears to be generally stable.

UTILIZATION: Badger fur is used for jackets and coat trimmings, and to make shaving brushes. Formerly the tough hides were made into rugs. In recent years the North American badger harvest has yielded 30 to 40 thousand pelts, valued at over one million dollars annually.

REFERENCES

BURT, W. H., and R. P. Grossenheider. 1964. A Field Guide to the Mammals. Houghton Mifflin Company, Boston. 289 pp.

DAVIS, W. B. 1946. Further Notes on Badgers. J. Mammal. 27: 175.

DEEMS, E. F., and D. Pursley. 1978. North American Furbearers, Their Management, Research and Harvest Status in 1976. International Association of Fish and Wildlife Agencies. 171 pp.

ERRINGTON, P.L. 1937. Summer Food Habits of the Badger in Northwestern Iowa. J. Mammal . 18: 213-216.

HALL, E. R. 1981. The Mammals of North America, Vol. II. John Wiley & Sons, Inc., New York. 118 pp.

HAMLETT, G. W. D. 1932. Observations on the Embryology of the Badger. Anatom. Rec. 53: 283-303.

HARLOW, J. H. 1981. Effect of Fasting on Rate of Food Passage and Assimulation Efficiency in Badgers. J. Mammal. 62: 173-177.

INGLES, L. G. 1947. Mammals of California. Stanford: Stanford University Press. pp. 72-77.

LAMPE, R. P. 1982. Food Habits of Badgers in East-Central Minnesota. J. Wildlife Management. (In press).

PETRIDES, G.A. 1950. The Determination of Sex and Age Ratios in Fur Animals. Am. Mid. Nat. 43: 355-382.

SAVODA. M. A. 1981. Seasonal Variation in Home Range of a Female Badger (*Taxidea taxus*). The Prairie Nat. 13 (2): 55-58.

SCHWARTZ, C.W., and E. R. Schwartz. 1964. The Wild Mammals of Missouri. Univ. of Missouri Press and Missouri Conservation Commission, Kansas City. 341 pp.

SNEAD, E., and G. O. Hendrickson. 1942. Food Habits of the Badger in Iowa. J. Mammal. 23: 380-391.

Map 21. **The Range of the Badger in the United States and Canada.**

Fig. 21

The Management Status of the Badger in the United States and Canada

STATES, PROVINCES AND TERRITORIES	Present	Total Protection	Hunting Season	Trapping Season	Year-Round Harvesting	Limited Harvesting	Food Resource	Habitat Management	Population Inventories	Special Regulations	Private Lands Leased
United States											
Alabama											
Alaska											
Arizona	●		●	●		●				●	
Arkansas	●		●	●		●					
California	●		●	●		●					
Colorado	●		●	●		●					
Connecticut											
Delaware											
Florida											
Georgia											
Idaho	●		●	●	●						
Illinois	●	●									
Indiana	●	●									
Iowa	●			●		●			●	●	
Kansas	●		●	●		●					
Kentucky											
Louisiana											
Maine											
Maryland											
Massachusetts											
Michigan	●	●									
Minnesota	●			●		●				●	
Mississippi											
Missouri	●		●	●		●			●	●	
Montana	●				●						
Nebraska	●				●						
Nevada	●				●						
New Hampshire											
New Jersey											
New Mexico	●			●		●					
New York											
North Carolina											

STATES, PROVINCES AND TERRITORIES	Present	Total Protection	Hunting Season	Trapping Season	Year-Round Harvesting	Limited Harvesting	Food Resource	Habitat Management	Population Inventories	Special Regulations	Private Lands Leased
United States (Cont'd)											
North Dakota	●		●	●	●						
Ohio	●		●								
Oklahoma	●		●	●		●			●		
Oregon	●			●	●						
Pennsylvania											
Rhode Island											
South Carolina											
South Dakota	●		●	●	●				●		
Tennessee											
Texas	●		●	●	●					●	
Utah	●				●						
Vermont											
Virginia											
Washington	●			●		●			●		
West Virginia											
Wisconsin	●	●									
Wyoming	●		●	●	●						
Total (United States)	26	4	12	18	10	11	0	0	5	5	0
Canada											
Alberta	●			●	●						
British Columbia	●	●									
Manitoba	●			●		●			●		
New Brunswick											
Newfoundland											
Northwest Territories											
Nova Scotia											
Ontario	●			●							
Prince Edward Island											
Quebec											
Saskatchewan	●		●	●		●					
Yukon Territory											
Total (Canada)	5	1	1	4	1	2	0	0	0	1	0

STRIPED SKUNK
(*Mephitis mephitis*)

DESCRIPTION: The striped skunk is about the size of a domestic cat. The triangular head tapers to a rounded, nearly ball-shaped nose pad. The ears are small and rounded and the small, beady, black eyes have no readily discernible pupils. The eyes do not have nictitating membranes (which is unique among carnivores). The body is thick, the legs are short and longer in the rear than in the front. The 5 toes on each front foot are equipped with long curved claws, whereas the 5 toes on each hind foot have shorter and straighter claws. The tail is long and bushy. The pelage is long, glossy and black, except for a narrow white stripe on the forehead and white stripe beginning on the head and extending to the shoulders, where it often divides into two stripes of variable length and width which may continue to the base of the tail. There may be some white hairs on the tail and the tips of the tail may be white. The black hairs on the tail are white at the base. There may be a white patch on the chest. Males and females are similar in appearance although males usually are somewhat larger. Adults range in length from 20 to 30 inches (51-76 cm) including the 7 to 10 inch (17-26 cm) tail and weigh from 3 1/2 to 10 pounds (2-5 kg). Skunks are equipped with 2 scent glands, one on each side of the anus, and are capable of spraying the musky effluvium produced by these glands for several yards. The skull has 34 teeth. There are 10 to 14 mammae.

HABITAT: The striped skunk is very adaptable and occurs throughout much of the U.S. (except Alaska) and Canada (except Newfoundland). They prefer semi-open country, such as forest borders, brushy field corners, fence rows and openlands, such as grassy fields and croplands interspersed with wooded ravines and rocky outcrops. Striped skunks are never far from a permanent water source, however, skunks do not remain long in areas where the water table frequently rises to within 2 or 3 feet of the soil's surface, thereby prohibiting the use of ground dens.

FEEDING HABITS: The omnivorous striped skunk eats a great variety of plant and animal material. Plants and animals are eaten during the fall and winter but animal matter is the primary food in spring and summer. Insects are preferred foods. Skunks dig and root in the soil for wasps, bees and their honey, larvae and hives and many other insects. Striped skunks also eat many kinds of crustaceans, amphibians, reptiles and their eggs, small mammals, birds and their eggs. Plant materials eaten include grasses, leaves, buds, roots, nuts, grain and fungi. Occasionally striped skunks depredate poultry houses eating both chickens and eggs.

BEHAVIOR: Striped skunks are primarily nocturnal but occasionally are abroad in the daytime. Their senses of smell and hearing are acutely developed. Striped skunks have relatively small home ranges, usually only 1/4 to 1/2 square mile (0.64-1.3 km²). Skunks are excellent diggers; among mustelids they are second only to the badger. Striped skunks den under brushpiles, rock piles, logs and buildings. Skunks do not hibernate but during cold weather they may stay in the den for as long as a month. Striped skunks generally are not social animals but they sometimes den with other skunks or other animals. As many as 20 skunks have been found in one den. Prior to spraying, skunks usually give warning signals by stamping their feet, gnashing their teeth, hissing, growling and raising their tails. Just before spraying, the back usually is bent in a U configuration with both head and tail facing the enemy.

REPRODUCTION: Striped skunks are promiscuous and usually breed in late February or early March. The gestation period is approximately 63 days. Litters contain 4 to 8 young. Females usually bear 4 young in their first litter and from 6 to 8 in subsequent litters. The altricial newborn weigh about 1 ounce (28 g), and their coat of fine hairs shows the adult patterns. The young are weaned in 6 to 7 weeks and during the latter part of this period the young follow the mother, in single file, on foraging trips. The young disperse in later summer or early fall. They are sexually mature and capable of breeding at one year of age.

POPULATION STATUS: North America's striped skunk population is stable and possibly increasing. Recent agricultural and land clearing practices have created new habitats and expanded striped skunk populations in some areas. Striped skunk are carriers of rabies and the reported number of rabid skunks has increased in the southeast and southwest in recent years.

UTILIZATION: The striped skunk primarily is sought and taken by fox trappers. Pelt values have been relatively low and stable for many years. The value of the pelt is inversely related to the amount of white markings. Mostly black pelts are more valuable. After the historic decline of the beaver, skunk effluvium was refined and used as a base for the most expensive perfumes. but since beaver have become numerous their castoreum has replaced skunk "essence" as a premium perfume base. In recent years the annual North American harvest of striped skunks has been 150 to 200 thousand pelts valued at 500 to 600 thousand dollars.

REFERENCES

BURT, W.H., and R.P. Grossenheider. 1964. A Field Guide to the Mammals. Houghton Mifflin Co., Boston. pp. 70-71.

DEEMS, E.F., and D. Pursley. 1978. North American Furbearers, Their Management, Research and Harvest Status in 1976. International Association of Fish and Wildlife Agencies. 171 pp.

LOWERY, G.H., Jr. 1974. The Mammals of Louisiana and its Adjacent Waters. Louisiana State University Press, Baton Rouge, Louisiana. pp. 438-445.

PALMER, R.S. 1954. The Mammal Guide. Doubleday and Company, Inc., Garden City, N.J. pp. 118-121.

SCHWARTZ, C.W., and E.R. Schwartz. 1959. The Wild Mammals of Missouri. Missouri Press, Columbia, Missouri. pp. 299-305.

SEALANDER, J.A. 1979. A Guide to Arkansas Mammals. River Road Press, Conway, Arkansas. pp. 235-237.

Map 22.

The Range of the Striped Skunk in the United States and Canada.

Fig. 22

The Management Status of the Striped Skunk in the United States and Canada

STATES, PROVINCES AND TERRITORIES	Present	Total Protection	Hunting Season	Trapping Season	Year-Round Harvesting	Limited Harvesting	Food Resource	Habitat Management	Population Inventories	Special Regulations	Private Lands Leased
United States											
Alabama	●		●		●					●	
Alaska	●										
Arizona	●		●	●		●				●	
Arkansas	●		●	●		●					
California	●			●	●						
Colorado	●		●	●	●						
Connecticut	●		●	●		●				●	
Delaware	●				●						
Florida	●				●					●	
Georgia	●			●		●				●	
Idaho	●		●	●	●						
Illinois	●		●	●		●			●	●	
Indiana	●			●		●			●		
Iowa	●			●		●			●	●	
Kansas	●		●	●	●						
Kentucky	●			●		●					
Louisiana	●			●		●					
Maine	●		●	●		●					
Maryland	●			●		●					
Massachusetts	●		●	●	●						
Michigan	●			●							
Minnesota	●			●						●	
Mississippi	●			●		●				●	
Missouri	●		●	●		●			●	●	
Montana	●				●						
Nebraska	●			●							
Nevada	●			●							
New Hampshire	●			●					●		
New Jersey	●			●		●			●		
New Mexico	●					●					
New York	●		●	●		●					
North Carolina	●			●		●					●

STATES, PROVINCES AND TERRITORIES	Present	Total Protection	Hunting Season	Trapping Season	Year-Round Harvesting	Limited Harvesting	Food Resource	Habitat Management	Population Inventories	Special Regulations	Private Lands Leased
United States (Cont'd)											
North Dakota	●		●	●	●						
Ohio	●		●								
Oklahoma	●		●	●		●			●		
Oregon	●			●	●						
Pennsylvania	●		●	●	●						
Rhode Island	●			●		●			●	●	
South Carolina	●		●	●		●				●	
South Dakota	●			●	●				●		
Tennessee	●		●	●		●					
Texas	●		●	●	●					●	
Utah	●			●							
Vermont	●			●		●					
Virginia	●			●	●						
Washington	●			●					●		
West Virginia	●		●	●	●						
Wisconsin	●		●	●	●						
Wyoming	●		●	●	●						
Total (United States)	48	0	20	37	24	23	0	0	10	13	1
Canada											
Alberta	●				●						
British Columbia	●		●	●	●						●
Manitoba	●			●	●					●	
New Brunswick	●		●	●					●		
Newfoundland											
Northwest Territories											
Nova Scotia	●		●	●							
Ontario	●			●	●						
Prince Edward Island	●		●	●	●						
Quebec	●			●	●						
Saskatchewan	●				●						
Yukon Territory											
Total (Canada)	9	0	4	7	7	0	0	0	1	1	1

SPOTTED SKUNK
(*Spilogale putorius*)

DESCRIPTION: The spotted skunk is similar to the striped skunk in appearance except spotted skunks are noticeably smaller, the body is slender and the color pattern is very distinctive. The overall color is black with a white spot on the forehead, one under each ear and 4 conspicuous broken white stripes along the neck, back and sides. The fur is long, soft and glossy. Both front and hind feet have 5 slightly webbed toes with moderately long claws. The sexes are alike in color and similar in size although males tend to be larger. Adults attain total lengths of 14 to 22 inches (36-56 cm) including the 5 to 9 inch (13-23 cm) tail, and weigh from ¾ to 2¾ pounds (0.35-1.25 kg). The skull has 34 teeth. There are 8 mammae.

HABITAT: The spotted skunk's habitat requirements are similar to those of the striped skunk — open prairies, cultivated fields and grassy fields associated with brushy field borders, fence rows or heavily vegetated gullies. They den below ground in grassy banks, rocky outcrops and along fence rows. They also den above ground in trees, brushpiles, hollow logs, haystacks, and buildings. Unlike the striped skunk, the spotted skunk is not well distributed throughout its range.

FEEDING HABITS: The spotted skunk's diet is similar to that of the striped skunk. Preferred insect foods include bees, wasps, grasshoppers, crickets, ground beetles and scarab beetles. Field mice are important and regular food items in winter. Occasionally rats and rabbits are taken. Birds and reptiles, as well as their eggs, occasionally are taken. Other food items include crayfish, salamanders, mushrooms, fruits, nuts and corn.

BEHAVIOR: Spotted skunks are nocturnal and are seldom active in the daytime. During most of the year a spotted skunk's home range usually is ¼ square mile (0.65 km²) or less in size but during the spring males, apparently restless, may range over a territory as large as 4 square miles (10 km²). Spotted skunks are excellent tree climbers and often will "tree" to escape dogs or other enemies. These skunks enter water (especially shallow water) readily. The spotted skunk's behavior immediately prior to and during the act of spraying is like that of the striped skunk — squeals, growls, hisses, snarls, teeth gnashing, feet stamping and back arched into a U shape. The odor of the spotted skunk's effluvium is similar to that of the striped skunk although some trappers and hunters maintain that the spotted skunk's is the more pungent and offensive.

REPRODUCTION: Breeding occurs in late winter. The young are born between April and July after a 60 to 63 day gestation period. In the deep south some females produce 2 litters in one year. Litters contain up to 7 young (usually 4 or 5). The altricial young weigh only ⅓ ounce (9 gm) at birth. Newborns are nearly naked but the black and white color pattern is evident on the skin. After 21 days the young are covered with dense fur and they are capable of spraying at 24 days of age. The half-grown young are weaned at about 54 days of age. Spotted skunks are full grown at 3½ to 4 months of age and usually breed during the first year.

POPULATION STATUS: The national spotted skunk population apparently has declined since the early 1900s. Spotted skunks are not as adaptable as striped skunks. Compared with striped skunks, spotted skunk populations are considerably more

171

localized or spotty in nature rather than generally distributed throughout the range.
UTILIZATION: Spotted skunks are taken primarily by trappers. Like striped skunks, spotted skunks are usually taken in conjunction with fox trapping efforts. And like striped skunks, spotted skunk pelt prices have remained relatively low but stable and the market for effluvium as a perfume base has been replaced by the beaver's castoreum. Recent annual U.S. harvests of spotted skunks have been 16 to 20 thousand pelts, averaging 4 to 6 dollars each.

REFERENCES

BURT, W.H., and R.P. Grossenheider. 1964. A Field Guide to the Mammals. Houghton Mifflin Co., Boston. 289 pp..

CRABB, W.D. 1941. Food Habits of the Prairie Spotted Skunk in Southeastern Iowa. J. Mammal. 22: 349-364.

_____. 1944. Growth, Development and Seasonal Weights of Spotted Skunks. J. Mammal. 25: 312-321.

_____. 1949. The Ecology and Management of the Prairie Spotted Skunk in Iowa. Ecol. Mono. 18: 201-232.

DEEMS, E.F., and D. Pursley. 1978. North American Furbearers, Their Management, Research and Harvest Status in 1976. International Association of Fish and Wildlife Agencies. 171 pp.

MEAD, R.A. 1966. Reproduction in the Spotted Skunk (*Spilogale putorius*). Ph.D. Thesis. Univ. Mont. 125 pp.

SCHWARTZ, C.W., and E.R. Schwartz. 1981. The Wild Mammals of Missouri. Univ. of Missouri Press and Missouri Conservation Commission, Kansas City. 356 pp.

Map 23.   **The Range of the Spotted Skunk in the United States and Canada.**

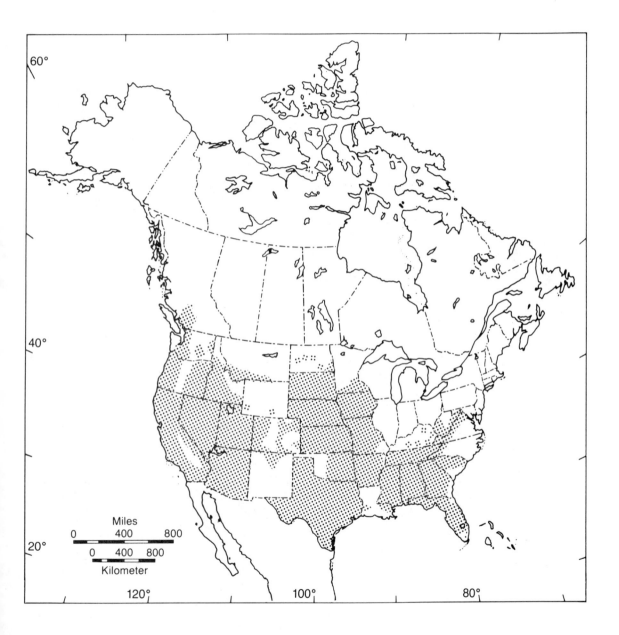

Fig. 23   **The Management Status of the Spotted Skunk in the United States and Canada**

STATES, PROVINCES AND TERRITORIES	Present	Total Protection	Hunting Season	Trapping Season	Year-Round Harvesting	Limited Harvesting	Food Resource	Habitat Management	Population Inventories	Special Regulations	Private Lands Leased
United States											
Alabama	●		●			●				●	
Alaska											
Arizona	●		●	●		●				●	
Arkansas	●		●	●		●					
California	●			●	●		●				
Colorado	●			●	●	●					
Connecticut											
Delaware											
Florida	●				●					●	
Georgia	●		●		●					●	
Idaho	●		●	●	●						
Illinois											
Indiana											
Iowa	●	●									
Kansas	●	●									
Kentucky	●			●		●					
Louisiana	●			●		●					
Maine											
Maryland	●			●		●					
Massachusetts											
Michigan											
Minnesota	●				●					●	
Mississippi	●			●		●				●	
Missouri	●		●	●		●			●	●	
Montana	●				●						
Nebraska	●	●									
Nevada	●			●							
New Hampshire											
New Jersey											
New Mexico	●					●					
New York											
North Carolina	●			●		●					●
United States (Cont'd)											
North Dakota	●		●	●							
Ohio											
Oklahoma	●		●	●	●						
Oregon	●			●	●						
Pennsylvania											
Rhode Island											
South Carolina	●		●	●		●				●	
South Dakota	●			●	●						
Tennessee	●		●	●		●					
Texas	●		●	●	●					●	
Utah	●			●							
Vermont											
Virginia	●			●	●				●		
Washington	●			●					●		
West Virginia	●		●	●	●						
Wisconsin											
Wyoming	●				●						
Total (United States)	33	3	11	22	15	15	0	0	4	9	1
Canada											
Alberta											
British Columbia	●		●	●	●						●
Manitoba											
New Brunswick											
Newfoundland											
Northwest Territories											
Nova Scotia											
Ontario											
Prince Edward Island											
Quebec											
Saskatchewan											
Yukon Territory											
Total (Canada)	1	0	1	1	1	0	0	0	0	0	1

RIVER OTTER
(*Lutra canadensis*)

DESCRIPTION: River otters have long slender bodies and short legs. The neck and shoulders are thick and well muscled, the feet are webbed, and the tail is long, tapered, and muscular. The head is broad with small ears, prominent eyes, and a short wide muzzle. The pelage varies from brown to almost black, however the chin, throat, cheeks, chest, and occasionally the belly are usually lighter, varying from brown to almost beige. The pelt contains relatively short guard hairs of uniform length that form a thick shiny outer coat which is underlain by shorter downy fur. The ends of the downy fur fibers are similar in color to the guard hairs, but they become lighter in color near the skin. Males are slightly larger than females. Adult males attain lengths of nearly 48 inches (122 cm) and weights of about 25 pounds (11.3 kg) whereas adult females reach lengths of about 44 inches (112 cm) and weights of about 19 pounds (8.6 kg). The skull has 36 teeth. There are 4 mammae.

HABITAT: River otters are almost invariably associated with water (fresh, brackish, and salt water), although they may travel overland for considerable distances. River otters inhabit lakes, rivers, streams, bays, estuaries, and the associated riparian habitats. The pre-colonial range of the river otter apparently included all of North America except the arid Southwest and the northernmost portions of Alaska and Canada. In colder climates otters frequent rapids and water-fall areas that remain ice-free. Vegetative cover and altitude do not appear to influence the river otter's distribution as much as do good or adequate water quality, availability of forage fish, and suitable denning sites.

FEEDING HABITS: The diet of the river otter is primarily fish, although shellfish, crayfish, amphibians, reptiles, and occasionally birds are taken. Nongame (rough) fish make up the major portion of a river otter's diet but game and pan fish also are taken.

BEHAVIOR: River otters are chiefly nocturnal, although they frequently are active during daylight hours. River otters spend much of their active time feeding and at what appears to be play, repeatedly sliding down steep banks of mud or snow. River otter vocalizations include chirps, grunts, and loud piercing screams. They are powerful swimmers. Their webbed feet, streamlined bodies, and long, tapered tails enable them to move through the water with agility, grace and speed. River otters may travel distances of 50 to 60 miles (80-96 km) along streams or lake shores and their home range may be as large as 60 square miles (155 km²).

REPRODUCTION: The reproductive biology of river otters is variable and they do not appear to synchronize their breeding or parturition seasons. Some studies indicate that river otters breed in the spring following parturition, whereas others suggest that females are receptive from December through early spring. One southeast study suggests that implantation may occur from late October to late February and that parturitions begin in late January, continue into March, and possibly occur as late as May. Studies at colder latitudes suggest March and April as birth months. River otters are promiscuous and pair bonding apparently does not occur. Gestation is about 60 to 65 days following implantation of the fertilized egg (blastocyst) that may have remained in the uterus in a free-floating state for 10 months. Litters usually contain 2 to 4 young although litters of 2 kits are more common than litters of 4. Sexual maturity is believed to occur at about 2 years of age in females, but male otters attain sexual maturity later than females. The female alone cares for the young and they usually remain together through the fall and into the winter months.

POPULATION STATUS: River otters are rare, or do not occur in several midwestern and great plains states and the southern half of the Canadian great plains provinces. Pesticide pollution, degredation or loss of wetland habitats, particularly those that disappeared when beaver were extirpated, and, more recently, acid rain and its effects on river otter foods are believed responsible for population losses in much of their former range. Restoration efforts have since returned dense beaver populations to much of the North American range and river otter are reinhabiting the new beaver-created wetlands, particularly in the Southeast. Reintroductions of river otter have high priority in some eastern and western mountainous states. Today river otters inhabit 43 states and all the Canadian provinces. They are totally protected in 17 states where the habitat is classified as secondary or transient range.

UTILIZATION: The river otter is both hunted and trapped but most are taken by trapping. Otter fur has long been considered a standard of durability and an example of quality in fur garments. It has commanded a relatively high and stable price even when most other furs were low in value. During the "fur boom" in the 1920s, river otter pelts were marketed for an average of about $31. The market value of otter pelts decreased in the following decade, but since that time market values of the river otter pelts appear to have generally paralled inflation rates. In recent years the annual North American harvests, and market values of river otter pelts have been relatively stable. About 50,000 river otter pelts valued at 1.5 to 3 million dollars are marketed annually.

REFERENCES

ANONYMOUS. 1977. Report of the Status of Canadian Used by the Fur Industry. Published by the Department of Industry, Trade & Commerce, Ottawa, Canada, in association with the Canada Fur Council.

BANFIELD, A.W.F. 1974. The Mammals of Canada. University of Toronto Press. 438 pp.

BURT, W.H. and R.P. Grossenheider. 1976. A Field Guide to the Mammals. 3rd Edition. Houghton Mifflin Co., Boston. 289 pp.

GREER, K.R. 1955. Yearly Food Habits of the River Otter in the Thompson Lakes Region, Northwestern Montana, as Indicated by Scat Analysis. Amer. Midl. Nat. 54(2): 299-313.

HALL, E.R. and K.R. Kelson. 1959. Mammals of North America. Ronald Press Co., New York, N.Y., 1083 pp.

HAMILTON, W.J., Jr. and W.R. Eadie. 1964. Reproduction in the Otter (*Lutra canadensis*). J. Mammal. 45(2): 242-252.

HILL, E.P. 1978. Current Harvest and Regulation of Trade of River Otters in the Southeastern United States in 1978. Pages 164-172. In Proc. Rare and Endangered Wildlife Symp. R. R. Odom and L. Landers, (eds.). Ga. Dept. Nat. Res. Game and Fish Div. Tech. Bul. WK 4. 184 pp.

_____, and V. Lauhachinda. 1981. Reproduction in River Otters from Alabama and Georgia. Pages 478-486. In Vol. II Worldwide Furbearer Conf. Proc. J.A. Chapman and D. Pursley, (eds.). Worldwide Furbearer Conference, Inc. Frostburg, Maryland.

HOOPER, E.T., and B.T. Ostenson. 1949. Age Groups in Michigan Otter. Occas. Pap. Mus. Zool.Univ., Michigan. No. 51. 22 pp.

KNUDSEN. G.J. 1962. Relationships of Beaver to Forest, Trout and Wildlife in Wisconsin. Wisconsin Cons. Dept. Bull. 25. 52 pp.

LAGLER, K.F., and B.T. Ostenson. 1942. Early Spring Food of the Otter in Michigan. J. Wildl. Manage. 6(3): 244-254.

LAUHACHINDA, V. 1978. Life History of the River Otter in Alabama with Emphasis on Food Habits. Ph.D. Dissertation, Auburn University. 185 pp.

_____, and E.P. Hill. 1977. Winter Food Habits of River Otters from Alabama and Georgia. Proc. Ann. Conf. S.E. Assoc. Fish & Wildl. Agencies. 31: 246-253.

LIERS, E.E. 1951. Notes on the River Otter (*Lutra canadensis*). J. Mammal. 32(1): 1-8.

MELQUIST, W.E. 1981. Ecological Aspects of a River Otter (*Lutra canadensis*). Population in West Central Idaho. Ph.D. Dissertation. Univ. of Idaho, Moscow. 170 pp.

MOWBRAY, E.E., D. Pursley and J.A. Chapman. 1979. The Status, Population Characteristics and Harvest of the River Otter in Maryland. Maryland Wildl. Admin., Publ. Wildl. Ecol. 2. 16 pp.

PARK, E. 1971. The World of the Otter. J. B. Lippincott Co., New York. 159 pp.

PETERSON, R.L. 1966. The Mammals of Eastern Canada. Toronto, Oxford University Press.

RYDER, R.A. 1954. Further Investigation of Fish Predation by Otter (*Lutra c. canadensis*), in Michigan. M.S. Thesis, University of Michigan. 15 pp.

SEVERINGHAUS, C.W., and J.E. Tanck. 1948. Speed and Gait of an Otter. J. Mammal. 29(1): 71.

SHELDON, W.G. and W.G. Toll. 1964. Feeding Habits of the River Otter in a Reservoir in Central Massachusetts. J. Mammal. 45(3): 449-455.

TABOR, J.E. 1974. Productivity, Survival, and Population Status of River Otter in Western Oregon. M.S. Thesis. Oregon State University. 62 pp.

TOLL, W.G. 1961. The Ecology of the River Otter (*Lutra canadensis*) in the Quabbin Reservation of Central Massachusetts. M. S. Thesis. University of Massachusetts. 45 pp.

TOWEILL, D.E. 1974. Winter Food Habits of River Otters in Western Oregon. J. Wildl. Manage. 38(1): 107-111.

WALKER, E.P. 1975. Mammals of the World (third ed.). Johns Hopkins Press, Baltimore, Maryland. 1500 pp.

WILSON, K.A. 1954. The Role of Mink and Otter as Muskrat Predators in Northeastern North Carolina. J. Wild. Manage. 18(2): 199-207.

Map 24. **The Range of the River Otter in the United States and Canada.**

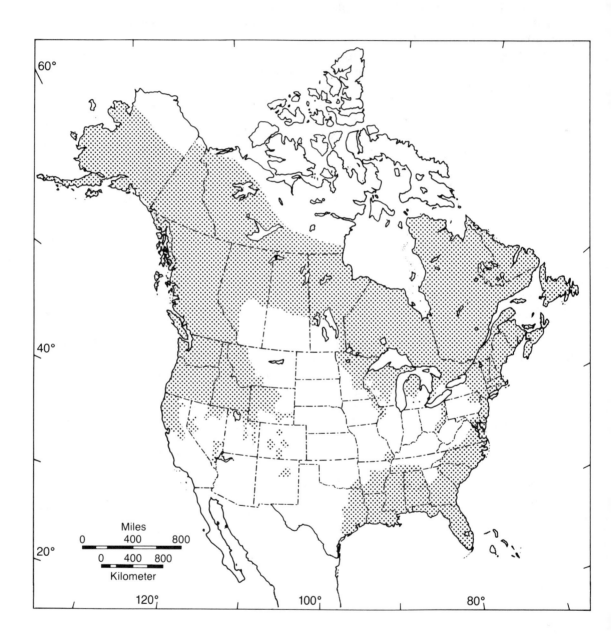

Fig. 24

The Management Status of the River Otter in the United States and Canada

STATES, PROVINCES AND TERRITORIES	Present	Total Protection	Hunting Season	Trapping Season	Year-Round Harvesting	Limited Harvesting	Food Resource	Habitat Management	Population Inventories	Special Regulations	Private Lands Leased
United States											
Alabama	●			●		●				●	
Alaska	●			●		●					
Arizona	●	●									
Arkansas	●		●	●		●					
California	●	●									
Colorado	●	●							●	●	
Connecticut	●			●				●	●	●	
Delaware	●			●							◐
Florida	●		●	●					●	●	
Georgia	●			●		●				●	
Idaho	●	●									
Illinois	●	●									
Indiana											
Iowa	●	●									
Kansas											
Kentucky											
Louisiana	●			●		●			●	●	●
Maine	●			●		●					
Maryland	●			●		●			●	●	●
Massachusetts	●			●		●				●	
Michigan	●			●		●					
Minnesota	●			●		●				●	
Mississippi	●			●		●				●	
Missouri	●	●									
Montana	●			●		●			●	●	
Nebraska											
Nevada	●			●		●			●		
New Hampshire	●			●		●			●	●	
New Jersey	●	●									
New Mexico	●	●									
New York	●			●		●			●		
North Carolina	●			●		●					
United States (Cont'd)											
North Dakota		●									
Ohio	●	●									
Oklahoma	●	●									
Oregon	●			●		●				●	
Pennsylvania	●	●							●		
Rhode Island	●	●				●			●	●	
South Carolina	●		●	●		●	●		●	●	
South Dakota											
Tennessee	●	●									
Texas	●		●	●	●				●	●	
Utah	●	●									
Vermont	●			●		●				●	
Virginia	●			●		●			●	●	
Washington	●			●		●			●		
West Virginia	●	●									
Wisconsin	●			●		●			●	●	●
Wyoming	●	●									
Total (United States)	43	18	4	26	1	24	1	1	16	19	4
Canada											
Alberta	●			●		●				●	●
British Columbia	●			●		●					
Manitoba	●			●		●				●	
New Brunswick	●			●		●			●		
Newfoundland	●			●		●					
Northwest Territories	●			●		●					
Nova Scotia	●		●	●		●					
Ontario	●			●		●			●		
Prince Edward Island	●	●									
Quebec	●			●		●					
Saskatchewan	●			●		●				●	
Yukon Territory	●			●		●				●	
Total (Canada)	12	1	1	11	0	11	0	0	2	4	1

COUGAR
(*Felis concolor*)

DESCRIPTION: The cougar (mountain lion) is the largest cat native to North America today. The head is relatively small, almost bullet shaped, and the face is short and rounded. The neck and body are elongate and narrow. The legs are very muscular and the hind legs are considerably longer than the forelegs. The tail is long, cylindrical and well haired. The pelage of the mountain lion varies considerably. There are two major color phases—red and gray. The red phase varies from buff, cinnamon and tawny to a very reddish color, while the gray phase varies from silvery gray to bluish and slate-gray. The sides of the muzzle are black. The upper lip, chin and throat are whitish. The tail is the same color as the body, except for the tip which is dark brown or black. The young are yellowish-brown with irregular rows of black spots. Male cougars usually are considerably larger than females. Adults range from 72 to 90 inches (183-229 cm) in total length including the tail, which is 30 to 36 inches (76-91 cm) long, and weigh from 80 to 200 pounds (36-91 kg). The skull has 30 teeth. There are 8 mammae.

HABITAT: The cougar inhabits a variety of habitats including coniferous forests, wooded swamps, tropical forests, open grasslands, chaparral, brushlands and desert edges. Its primary range occurs in western Canada and in the western and southeastern states in the United States. Cougars apparently prefer rough, rocky, semi-open areas, but show no particular preference for vegetation types.

FEEDING HABITS: Cougars are carnivorous. Their diet varies according to habitat, season and geographical region. The main prey species is deer, but other prey species range from moose to mice, including elk, bear cubs, antelope, mountain sheep, Rocky Mountain goats, beaver, peccaries, aplodontia (boomers), hares, rabbits, porcupines, coyotes, martens, skunks, wild turkeys, grouse, fish, occasionally domestic livestock and pets, and even insects. Cougars, like bobcats and lynx, are sometimes cannibalistic.

BEHAVIOR: Mountain lions are shy, elusive and primarily nocturnal animals that occasionally are active during daylight hours. They attain great running speeds for short distances and they are agile tree climbers. The cougar generally is solitary. Its home range usually is 12 to 22 square miles (31-57 km²) although it may travel distances of 75 to 100 miles (120-161 km) from the place of birth.

REPRODUCTION: The cougar does not have a definite breeding season, and mating may take place at anytime. In North America there are records of births in every month, although the majority of births occur in late winter and early spring. The female is in estrus for approximately 9 days. After a gestation period of 90 to 96 days, a litter of 1 to 5 altricial young (usually 3 or 4), are born. The kittens can eat meat at six weeks of age, although they usually nurse until about 3 months of age. The young usually hunt with their mother through their first winter.

POPULATION STATUS: Historically, the North American cougar population was drastically reduced by the encroachment of civilization and the resultant habitat destruction. The present cougar population apparently is stable and viable. Local populations may fluctuate in response to changes in prey populations, particularly deer, the primary food source.

UTILIZATION: The cougar is hunted primarily as a trophy animal. Trail and sight hounds are used. Pelts usually are used for trophy mounts and rugs. The claws and teeth are used for jewelry and novelty ornaments. The cougar is not an important species in the fur trade. In North America cougars are primarily harvested in Arizona, British Columbia and Alberta. Arizona provides the majority of the 200 to 300 cougars harvested annually.

REFERENCES

ANONYMOUS. 1978. Report on the Status of Canadian Wildlife Used by the Fur Industry. Dept. of Industry, Trade and Commerce, Ottawa. 66 pp.

_____. 1979. Fur Production, 1977-78. Statistics Canada, Ottawa. 17 pp.

BANFIELD. A.W.F. 1974. The Mammals of Canada. Univ. of Toronto Press. 438 pp.

BURT, W.H., and R.P. Grossenheider. 1964. A Field Guide to the Mammals. Houghton Mifflin Co., Boston, Mass. pp. 82-84.

COWAN, I. McTaggart and C.J. Guiguet. 1965. The Mammals of British Columbia. Queens Printer, Victoria, B.C. 414 pp.

DEEMS, E.F., and D. Pursley. 1978. North American Furbearers, Their Management, Research and Harvest Status in 1976. International Association of Fish and Wildlife Agencies. 171 pp.

GRIGGISBERG, C.A.W. 1975. Wildcats of the World. Taplinger Publishing Company, New York, New York. pp. 107-124.

HORNOCKER, Maurice. 1976. Biology and Life History. Pages 38-91, in G.C. Christensen and R.J. Fischer, eds. Trans. Mountain Lion Workshop, Sparks, Nevada.

LOWERY, G.H., Jr. 1974. The Mammals of Louisiana and its Adjacent Waters. Louisiana State University Press, Baton Route, Louisiana. pp. 456-466.

PALMER, R.S. 1954. The Mammal Guide. Doubleday and Company, Inc., Garden City, N.J. pp. 141-143.

PETERSON, Randolph L. 1973. The Mammals of Eastern Canada. Oxford Univ. Press, Toronto. 465 pp.

SCHWARTZ, C.W., and E.R. Schwartz. 1959. The Wild Mammals of Missouri. University of Missouri Press, Columbia, Missouri. p. 332.

SEALANDER, J.A. 1979. A Guide to Arkansas Mammals. River Road Press, Conway, Arkansas. pp. 241-245.

SHAW, Harley. 1976. Depredation. Pages 145-176, in G.C. Christensen and R. J. Fischer, eds. Trans. Mountain Lion Workshop, Sparks, Nevada.

Map 25. The Range of the Cougar in the United States and Canada.

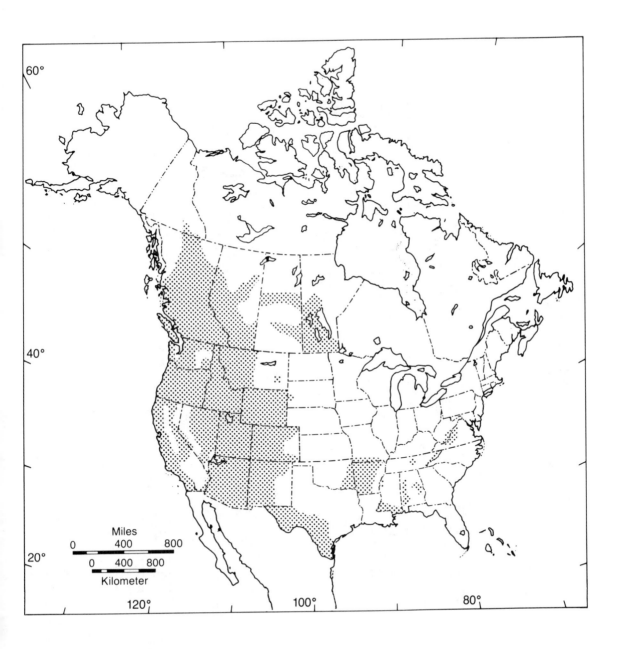

Miles
0   400   800

0   400   800
Kilometer

Fig. 25   **The Management Status of the Cougar in the United States and Canada**

STATES, PROVINCES AND TERRITORIES	Present	Total Protection	Hunting Season	Trapping Season	Year-Round Harvesting	Limited Harvesting	Food Resource	Habitat Management	Population Inventories	Special Regulations	Private Lands Leased
United States											
Alabama	●	●									
Alaska											
Arizona	●				●		●	●	●		
Arkansas	●	●									
California	●	●							●	●	
Colorado	●		●			●				●	
Connecticut		●									
Delaware											
Florida	●	●									
Georgia	●	●									
Idaho	●		●			●			●	●	
Illinois											
Indiana											
Iowa											
Kansas											
Kentucky											
Louisiana	●	●									
Maine											
Maryland											
Massachusetts											
Michigan											
Minnesota											
Mississippi	●	●									
Missouri											
Montana	●		●			●			●	●	
Nebraska											
Nevada	●		●			●			●	●	
New Hampshire			●							●	
New Jersey											
New Mexico	●		●			●			●		
New York											
North Carolina	●	●									
United States (Cont'd)											
North Dakota	●	●									
Ohio											
Oklahoma	●	●							●		
Oregon	●		●			●			●	●	
Pennsylvania											
Rhode Island											
South Carolina											
South Dakota	●	●									
Tennessee	●	●									
Texas	●				●						
Utah	●		●			●					
Vermont											
Virginia	●	●									
Washington	●		●			●			●		
West Virginia	●	●									
Wisconsin											
Wyoming	●		●		●				●		
Total (United States)	25	16	10	0	3	8	1	1	10	7	0
Canada											
Alberta	●		●			●				●	
British Columbia	●		●		●	●					
Manitoba	●	●									
New Brunswick	●	●									
Newfoundland											
Northwest Territories											
Nova Scotia		●									
Ontario											
Prince Edward Island											
Quebec											
Saskatchewan	●	●									
Yukon Territory											
Total (Canada)	5	4	2	0	1	2	0	0	0	1	0

LYNX
(*Felis canadensis*)

DESCRIPTION: The lynx is a short-tailed cat (like the bobcat) that is easily distinguished by its long legs, disproportionately large and furry snowshoe-like feet with retractable claws. The face has a prominent gray ruff and the ears are very large and prominently tipped with long black tufts. The tail is short (4 inches or 10-12 cm) and blunt with a black tip which completely encircles the tail. The thick and luxurious pelage is generally light gray and grizzled with brown, darker on head and back where guard hairs are subterminally white with terminal brown or black tips. The winter coat is long and greyish white while the summer coat is browner and shorter. Sexes are similar in appearance except males are larger than females. Adults weigh 16 to 40 pounds (7.3-18.1 kg) and reach 34 to 40 inches (86-102 cm) in length. The skull has 28 teeth. There are 4 mammae.

HABITAT: The lynx inhabits the boreal forest belt across Canada. It also hunts on the tundra beyond the treeline. With the exception of Prince Edward Island, it occurs in every Canadian province. Habitat types include northern coniferous forests, mixed coniferous-hardwood forest and birch-aspen communities in the taiga-subalpine life zones. Lynx occasionally travel to forested areas as far south as Iowa and Indiana although the southern distribution of their range appears to be receding northward.

FEEDING HABITS: The primary prey species is the snowshoe hare. Lynx also eat grouse, ptarmigans, porcupines, squirrels, deer, beaver, mice and other small mammals. Lynx prefer live prey to carrion but will eat carrion if food is scarce. Since little domestic livestock is raised in the primary lynx range, depradations are rare, but lynx occasionally kill and eat sheep, poultry and household pets when they are available.

BEHAVIOR: Lynx primarily are nocturnal. Females will travel with their kittens but adult males tend to be solitary. Lynx are known to range widely up to 300 miles (482.8 km) especially during "crashes" in local snowshoe hare population levels. The lynx is an excellent swimmer and tree climber. Apparently lynx are not strongly competitive with other predators. The lynx has been replaced in some parts of its historic range by bobcats and coyotes. The senses of sight and hearing are acutely developed in the lynx. Lynx den in hollow logs, under deadfall roots and trees, and in other sheltered aeas.

REPRODUCTION: Lynx are promiscuous. The mating season is January through March. The gestation period is about 62 days. Litters contain 1 to 4 (usually 2 or 3) altricial young. The kittens are reared by their mother only and are dependent on her for 9 months or longer. Lynx apparently breed in their second year.

POPULATION STATUS: North America's lynx population is currently stable or increasing in the primary range in Alaska and Canada (excluding some Maritime Provinces). In the northern and Rocky Mountain states where lynx range is peripheral the local population levels are directly affected by the ingress and egress of lynx from the primary habitats in Canada. Lynx population levels exhibit definite cyclic characteristics, peaking approximately every 10 years in a direct but lagging relationship with snowshoe hare population cycles. Lynx either starve or disperse into new territories during snowshoe hare population declines and "crash" periods.

UTILIZATION: Lynx are taken by both trappers and hunters. Hunting with hounds is a traditional recreation in some areas but many hunters prefer to hunt lynx alone while traveling on skis or snowshoes. Lynx pelts are used in full garments and for trimmings and accessories. Teeth and claws are used in jewelry. Lynx meat, considered a delicacy, is commonly eaten by hunters and trappers in Canada and Alaska. In recent years the North American lynx harvest has averaged over 20,000 pelts per year for total market values of more than 6 million dollars annually. This production will undoubtedly continue to fluctuate with the lynx and hare cycles.

REFERENCES

ANONYMOUS. 1978. Report on the Status of Canadian Wildlife Used by the Fur Industry. Dept. of Industry, Trade and Commerce, Ottawa. 66 pp.

_____. 1979. Fur Production, 1977-78. Statistics Canada, Ottawa. 17 pp.

ANTHONY, H.E. 1952. Animals of the World. Garden City Books, Garden City, New York. 354 pp.

ARMSTRONG, D.M. 1972. Distribution of Mammals in Colorado. Mus. of Nat. Hist., The Univ. of Kansas, Monogr. No. 3. 415 pp.

BANFIELD, A.W.F. 1974. The Mammals of Canada. Univ. of Toronto Press. 438 pp.

BERRIE, P.M. 1972. Sex Differences in Response to Phencyclidine Hydrochloride in Lynx. J. Wildl. Manage. 36(3): 994-996.

BRAND, C.J., L.B. Keith and C.A. Fischer. 1976. Lynx Responses to Changing Snowshoe Hare Densities in Central Alberta. J. Wildl. Manage. 40(3): 416-428.

BURT, W.H., and R.P. Grossenheider. 1964. A Field Guide to the Mammals. Houghton Mifflin Co., Boston. 289 pp.

COWAN, I. McTaggart, and C.J. Guiguet. 1965. The Mammals of British Coumbia. Queens Printer, Victoria, B.C. 414 pp.

DEEMS, E.F., and D. Pursley. 1978. North American Furbearers, Their Management, Research and Harvest Status in 1976. International Association of Fish and Wildlife Agencies. 171 pp.

GUNDERSON, H.A. 1978. Midcontinent Irruption of Canada Lynx. 1962-63. Prairie Nat. 10(30: 71-80.

HALL, E.R., and K.R. Kelson. 1959. The Mammals of North America. Ronald Press Co., New York. 1083 pp.

HENDERSON, C. 1978. The Lynx Link. DNR Reports. Minn. Dept. of Nat. Res., 350 Centennial Off. Bldg., St. Paul, Minn., 55155. #74.

JACKSON, H.H.T. 1972. Mammals of Wisconsin. Univ. of Wis. Press, Madison. pp. 395-400.

KEITH, L.B. 1977. Canada Lynx. Canadian Wildlife Service, Dept. of Fisheries and the Environment, Ottawa. 3 pp.

MECH, L.D. 1977. Record Movement of a Canadian Lynx. J. Mammal. 58(4): 676-677.

NELLIS, C.H., and L.B. Keith. 1968. Hunting Activities and Success of Lynxes in Alberta. J. Wildl. Manage. 32(4): 718-722.

_____, and S.P. Wetmore. 1969. Long-range Movement of Lynx in Alberta. J. Mammal. 50(3): 640.

PARKER, G. 1978. Lynx Study Cape Breton Island. N.S. Trappers Newsletter. No. 14, Oct. 1978. pp. 10-11.

PETERSON, Randolph L. 1973. The Mammals of Eastern Canada. Oxford Univ. Press, Toronto. 465 pp.

Map 26.   **The Range of the Lynx in the United States and Canada.**

Fig. 26

The Management Status of the Lynx in the United States and Canada

STATES, PROVINCES AND TERRITORIES	Present	Total Protection	Hunting Season	Trapping Season	Year-Round Harvesting	Limited Harvesting	Food Resource	Habitat Management	Population Inventories	Special Regulations	Private Lands Leased
United States											
Alabama											
Alaska	●		●	●		●	●				
Arizona											
Arkansas											
California											
Colorado	●	●							●		
Connecticut											
Delaware											
Florida											
Georgia											
Idaho	●		●	●		●			●	●	
Illinois											
Indiana											
Iowa											
Kansas											
Kentucky											
Louisiana											
Maine	●	●									
Maryland											
Massachusetts											
Michigan	●	●									
Minnesota	●		●	●		●			●	●	
Mississippi											
Missouri											
Montana	●		●	●		●			●	●	
Nebraska											
Nevada											
New Hampshire	●	●								●	
New Jersey											
New Mexico											
New York			●								
North Carolina											
North Dakota	●		●	●		●			●		
Ohio											
Oklahoma											
Oregon											
Pennsylvania											
Rhode Island											
South Carolina											
South Dakota											
Tennessee											
Texas											
Utah	●	●									
Vermont	●	●									
Virginia											
Washington	●			●		●				●	
West Virginia											
Wisconsin	●	●									
Wyoming	●	●									
Total (United States)	14	9	5	6	0	6	1	0	5	5	0
Canada											
Alberta	●			●		●	●			●	
British Columbia	●		●	●		●	●				●
Manitoba	●			●		●	●			●	
New Brunswick	●	●									
Newfoundland	●			●		●	●				
Northwest Territories	●			●		●	●				
Nova Scotia	●		●	●		●	●		●	●	
Ontario	●			●		●			●		
Prince Edward Island											
Quebec	●		●	●		●					
Saskatchewan	●			●						●	
Yukon Territory	●			●		●	●			●	
Total (Canada)	11	1	3	10	0	9	7	0	2	5	1

BOBCAT
(*Lynx rufus*)

DESCRIPTION: The bobcat is a stout-bodied, medium-sized cat with a short tail, prominent face ruff, and tufts of black hair on its pointed ears. Although pelage coloration varies geographically, prominent white dots on the dorsal surface of the ears occur range-wide. The sides and flanks usually are brownish black or reddish brown with distinct or faint black spots. The back usually is tawny with a dark mid-dorsal line. Southern specimens often exhibit a yellowish or reddish cast on their backs and necks. The belly and inside of the legs usually are whitish gray with black spots whereas the chest and outside of the legs are brownish with black spotting or bars. Pelage tends to be longer in high elevations, northern states, and Canada than in more temperate areas. The tail is a little longer than that of the lynx and is characterized by one to several indistinct dark bands and a tip that is black on top and whitish below. The most distinctly colored specimens come from the Colorado-Montana area, the Pacific northwest and Nova Scotia. Male bobcats tend to be larger than females. Adult males range from 31.5 to 34.5 inches (80-88 cm) long and weigh from 14 to 40 pounds (6.4 - 18 kg). Adult females range from 28 to 31.7 inches (71 - 81 cm) in length and weigh from 9 to 33 pounds (4 - 15 kg). Records indicate a tendency for bobcats to be heavier along the northern portions of the range and in western states at medium altitudes. The skull has 28 teeth. There are 6 mammae.

HABITAT: The bobcat is tolerant, highly adaptable, and occurs in a wide variety of habitats, temperature, and altitude conditions. Unlike the lynx, which prefers unbroken forested areas, the bobcat seems to thrive in areas where there is an interspersion of mixed ground cover and openings. Bobcats appear to benefit from limited human activity and have extended their range into southern Canada as scattered agricultural openings were created in the extensive forestlands.

FEEDING HABITS: Bobcats are opportunistic carnivores that feed upon a wide variety of animals including live kills and carrion but specialize in hunting rabbit-sized prey. As much as 87% of the bobcat's diet is composed of hares, rabbits, and rodents, including rats and mice, tree squirrels and ground squirrels, porcupines, aplodontia (boomers), gopher, and ground hogs. In Canada the snowshoe hare is a primary prey species of the bobcat. Other food includes deer, opossums, raccoons, grouse, wild turkeys and other birds and, to a much lesser extent, insects and reptiles. Domestic prey species include small pigs, sheep, goats, poultry, and house cats. Bobcats occasionally kill and eat other bobcats, generally kittens.

BEHAVIOR: Bobcats are active at all times but tend to be nocturnal and crepuscular, exhibiting higher activity periods just after dark and before dawn. Bobcats are secretive, shy, solitary, and seldom seen in the wild. They tend to travel well worn animal trails, logging roads, and other paths, relying primarily on their keen eyesight and hearing for locating enemies and prey. The bobcat's sense of smell is not acute. They are territorial and their home ranges can vary from 0.4 to 15.8 square miles (0.9 to 42.1 km²) in area. Daily movements of 1 to 4 miles (2 - 7 km) are common. Females tend to have smaller and more exclusive ranges than males.

REPRODUCTION: Bobcats are polygamous and do not form lasting pair bonds. Breeding occurs primarily between January and June. The gestation period is estimated to be 50 to 70 days. Litters contain from 2 to 4 kittens and kitten survival is a primary factor in annual bobcat population fluctuations. Males do not participate in raising the young. Kittens nurse for about 60 days and accompany their mother through their first winter. Females are seasonally polyestrus and may breed before they are one year old. Males are fertile year-round but do not breed until their second winter.

POPULATION STATUS: In the southeast, bobcats attain densities of about 1 bobcat per ¼ square mile on some of the Gulf Coastal Islands. Densities vary from about 1 per ½ square mile in the coastal plains to about one cat per 4 square miles in portions of the Appalachian foothills. In Canada and the northern and western U.S., bobcat population levels tend to be influenced more by cyclic fluctuations in prey densities. Bobcats reportedly are scarce in midwestern and mid-Atlantic coastal states, where habitat destruction associated with intensive agricultural and other human land uses are the major limiting factors.

UTILIZATION: Bobcats are taken by trappers and by hunters using hounds. The pelts are used for coats, trim, and accessories and the spotted belly fur is most valuable. Bobcat pelts are used for wall decorations and rugs. The meat is considered to be excellent for human consumption although not widely utilized. In recent years, the North American bobcat harvests have produced about 80,000 pelts valued at approximately 11 million dollars annually. Esthetically the bobcat is a highly regarded carnivore because to many people the bobcat represents the essence of wildness in any habitat it occupies.

REFERENCES

ASDELL, S.A. 1964. Patterns of Mammalian Reproduction. Comstock Pub. Co., Ithaca, New York. vii + 670 pp.

BAILEY, T.N. 1972. Ecology of Bobcats with Special Reference to Social Organization. Ph.D. Thesis. Univ. of Idaho. 82 p.

_____. 1974. Social Organization in a Bobcat Population. J. Wildl. Manage. 38(3): 435-446.

CROWE, D.M. 1974. Some Aspects of Reproduction and Population Dynamics of Bobcats in Wyoming. Ph.D. Thesis. Univ. of Wyoming. 191 p.

_____. 1975. Aspects of Aging, Growth and Reproduction of Bobcats from Wyoming. J. Mammal. 56(1): 177-198.

DUKE, K.L. 1954. Reproduction in the Bobcat *Lynx rufus*. Anat. Rec. 120 (3): 816-817.

ERICKSON. A. W. 1955. An Ecological Study of the Bobcat in Michigan. M. S. Thesis. Mich. State Univ. 133 pp.

EWER, R. F. 1973. The Carnivores. Cornell Univ. Press. Ithaca, New York, xv + 494 pp.

FRITTS, S. H. 1973. Age, Food Habits, and Reproduction of the Bobcat *(Lynx rufus)* in Arkansas. M. S. Thesis, Univ. Ark. 80 p.

_____, and J. A. Sealander. 1978. Reproductive Biology and Population Characteristics of Bobcats *(Lynx rufus)* in Arkansas. J. Mammal. 59(2): 347-353.

GASHWILER, J. S., W. L. Robinette and O. W. Morris. 1961. Breeding Habits of Bobcats in Utah. J. Mammal. 42 (1): 76-84.

HALL, H. T. 1973. An Ecological Study of the Bobcat in Southeastern Louisiana.

Master's Thesis. LSU Baton Rouge. 132 pp.

_____, and J. D. Newsom. 1976. Summer Home Ranges and Movements of Bobcats in Bottomland Hardwoods of Southern Louisiana. Proc. Ann. Conf. S.E. Assoc. Fish and Wildl. Agencies. 30: 427-736.

MARSHALL, A. D., AND J. H. Jenkins. 1966. Movements and Home Ranges of Bobcats as Determined by Radio-tracking in the Upper Coastal Plain of West-central South Carolina. Proc. Ann. Conf. S.E. Assoc. Game and Fish Comm. 20: 206-214.

McCHORD, C. M. 1973. Courtship Behavior in Free-ranging Bobcats. In R. L. Eaton (ed.), The World's Cats, Volume II, Biology, Behavior and Management of Reproduction, Feline Research Group, Seattle, pp. 76-87.

_____. 1974. Selection of Winter Habitat by Bobcats (*Lynx rufus*) on the Quabbin Reservation, Massachusetts. J. Mammal. 55(2): 428-437.

MILLER, S. D. 1980. The Ecology of the Bobcat in South Alabama, Ph.D. Dissertation, Auburn Univ. Aunburn, Ala. 156 pp.

_____, and D. W. Speake. 1978. Prey Utilization by Bobcats on Quail Plantations in South Alabama. Proc. Ann. Conf. S.E. Assoc. Fish and Wildl. Agencies. 32: 100-111.

POLLACK, E. M. 1949. The Ecology of the Bobcat (*Lynx rufus rufus* Schreber) in the New England States. M. S. Thesis. Univ. of Mass. 120 p.

_____. 1950. Breeding Habits of the Bobcat in the Northeastern United States. J. Mammal. 31(3): 327-330.

PROGULSKE, D. R. 1952. The Bobcat and its Relation to Prey Species in Virginia, M. S. Thesis. VA Polytechnic Inst. 135 p.

PROVOST, E. E., C. A. Nelson and D.A. Marshall. 1973. Population Dynamics Behavior in the Bobcat. pages 42-67 in R. L. Eaton (ed.), The World's Cats, I: Ecology and Conservation. World Wildlife Safari, Winston, Oregon. 349 p.

ROLLINGS, C. T. 1942. Habits, Foots and Parasites of the Bobcat in Minnesota. M. S. Thesis. Univ. of Minnesota. 66 p.

SHELDON W. G. 1959. A Late Breeding Record of a Bobcat in Massachusetts. J. Mammal. 40 (1): 148.

SWEENEY. S. 1977. A Contribution Towards an Annotated Bibliography on the Bobcat (*Lynx rufus*) and Canada Lynx (*Lynx canadensis*). Final Job Report for Job 1. Studies II and III, W-84-R-4. Washington game Dept. Olympia. 55 p.

YOUNG, S. P. 1958. The Bobcat of North America. Stackpole Co., Harrisburg, Pa., and Wildl. Manage. Inst., Washington, D.C. 193 pp.

Fig. 27 **The Management Status of the Bobcat in the United States and Canada**

STATES, PROVINCES AND TERRITORIES	Present	Total Protection	Hunting Season	Trapping Season	Year-Round Harvesting	Limited Harvesting	Food Resource	Habitat Management	Population Inventories	Special Regulations	Private Lands Leased
United States											
Alabama	●		●	●		●				●	
Alaska											
Arizona	●		●	●		●				●	
Arkansas	●		●	●		●					
California	●		●	●		●			●		
Colorado	●		●	●		●				●	
Connecticut	●	●									
Delaware											
Florida	●		●	●					●	●	
Georgia	●		●	●		●			●	●	
Idaho	●		●	●		●			●	●	
Illinois	●	●									
Indiana	●	●									
Iowa	●	●									
Kansas	●		●	●		●			●	●	
Kentucky	●	●									
Louisiana	●			●		●			●		
Maine	●		●	●		●			●	●	
Maryland	●	●									
Massachusetts	●		●	●		●				●	
Michigan	●		●	●		●		●	●	●	
Minnesota	●		●	●		●			●	●	
Mississippi	●			●		●			●	●	
Missouri	●	●							●	●	
Montana	●		●	●		●			●	●	
Nebraska	●		●	●		●			●	●	
Nevada	●		●	●		●			●		
New Hampshire	●	●							●		
New Jersey	●	●									
New Mexico	●					●			●	●	
New York	●		●	●		●			●		
North Carolina	●		●	●		●			●		●
United States (Cont'd)											
North Dakota	●		●	●	●						
Ohio	●	●									
Oklahoma	●		●	●		●			●		
Oregon	●		●	●		●					
Pennsylvania	●	●									
Rhode Island	●	●								●	
South Carolina	●		●	●		●	●		●	●	
South Dakota	●		●	●		●			●		
Tennessee	●		●	●		●			●		
Texas	●				●				●	●	
Utah	●	●							●		
Vermont	●		●	●		●			●		
Virginia	●		●	●		●			●	●	
Washington	●		●	●		●			●		
West Virginia	●		●	●		●			●		
Wisconsin	●		●	●		●			●	●	
Wyoming	●		●	●	●						
Total (United States)	47	13	30	32	3	30	1	1	29	21	1
Canada											
Alberta	●		●	●						●	
British Columbia	●			●	●	●					●
Manitoba	●			●		●				●	
New Brunswick	●		●	●					●		
Newfoundland											
Northwest Territories											
Nova Scotia	●		●	●					●		
Ontario	●			●		●			●		
Prince Edward Island											
Quebec	●		●	●	●						
Saskatchewan	●			●	●						
Yukon Territory											
Total (Canada)	8	0	4	8	3	3	0	0	3	2	1

SECTION IV
ORDER PINNIPEDIA

Fur seal bull (center) is surrounded by harem of cows.

NORTHERN FUR SEAL
(*Callorhinus ursinus*)

DESCRIPTION: Northern fur seals are smaller than hooded seals and larger than harp seals. Their fur is incredibly dense (300,000 hairs per square inch) and impermeable to water. The pelage color varies considerably. Young males and females appear black when wet and gray when dry. Newborn pups are black but turn gray at about 2 months of age (during their first molt). Older males (6 years and older) vary in color from brownish-black to dark gray or reddish-brown. After 6 years of age, the males develop a short bushy mane on their shoulders and neck. Males are considerably larger than females. Adult males reach 94 inches (213 cm) in length and weigh up to 700 pounds (318 kg) while adult females reach 56 inches (142 cm) in length and weigh up to 130 pounds (59 kg). Unlike the hooded and harp seals, the northern fur seals' hind feet (flippers) can be turned forward so they can walk on land. The skull has 36 interlocking teeth. There are 2 mammae.

HABITAT: The northern fur seal is a migratory marine mammal that occurs in the North Pacific Ocean. It is the only fur seal that ranges along a U.S. coast. Northern fur seals travel in migratory routes that extend down both sides of the North Pacific Ocean to approximately 32 degrees North Latitude. In the Western Pacific Ocean, they range from the Commander Islands to areas southwest of Tokyo and into the seas of Japan and Okhotsk. On the eastern side, fur seals migrate as far south as the Channel Islands off the coast of Santa Barbara, California. These seals usually occur in waters that are 10 to 100 miles (16 - 161 km) offshore and most range in areas that are 30 to 70 miles (48 - 113 km) offshore.

FEEDING HABITS: The northern fur seal is an opportunistic carnivore that feeds primarily on fish (about 80%) and squid (about 20%). Fish taken include capelin, sandlance, pollock and herring. Feeding habits vary throughout the range depending on prey availability and fur seal activities. Northern fur seals compete with fishermen from several nations for some species of fish, such as pollock, and squid. Fish consumption by northern fur seals in the Aleutian Island area and Eastern Bering Sea, in summer months, is an estimated 2% of the standing stock annually compared to the 5% harvested by commercial fishermen each year. Northern fur seals feed on at least 54 species of fish and 9 species of squid.

BEHAVIOR: Northern fur seals primarily are nocturnal feeders since many of their prey species rise to upper water layers during darkness. The seal's eyes are relatively large and well adapted for night vision. There is a considerable amount of intermixing between northern fur seals from American and Asian Islands. Apparently 20 to 30 percent of the fur seals of ages 3 to 5 years that occur off the coast of Japan in winter and spring each year come from Alaska's Pribilof Islands. Males seals from the Commander Islands comprise about one percent of the annual bachelor seal harvest on the Pribilofs. Unless sick or injured, fur seals rarely touch land in the late fall-winter-early spring period. Depending on their age and sex, fur seals arrive at their rookery islands in the late spring to early summer period and leave in the late summer to early fall period. Fur seals often sleep on the ocean's surface, floating on their sides or backs, with all 4 flippers folded or with one or more stretched into the air. However, on the rookeries, fur seals are active continually. The big breeding males arrive at the Pribilof rookeries in late May or early June and each immediately establishes his own individual territory. Each of the beach masters (breeding males) attempts to intercept as many of the arriving mature females as he can and herd them into his own private harem within his individual territory. Beach masters frequently engage in savage battles and by the end of the breeding season (late summer) they have lost most of the stored fat (blubber) they had on arrival.

REPRODUCTION: Northern fur seals are polygamous. Breeding males may service as many as 100 females. Females become sexually mature at 3 to 5 years of age and enter the breeding population soon thereafter. Males become sexually mature at 4 to 5 years of age but they are not large and strong enough to establish territories and defend harems until they are about 10 years old. Single pups are born within 3 days of the pregnant females' arrival on the rookies. Harem females breed immediately (within 5 days) post partum, but implanatation of the blastocyst is delayed until November. Adult male fur seals arrive on the rookeries in late May and early June while females arrive about one month later. Adults leave the rookeries and return to the sea in September and October. Young of the year leave the rookeries in October and November and do not usually return to their rookeries until they are about 2 years old.

POPULATION STATUS: The northern fur seal and the harp seal are the most abundant fur seals in the world. The population of the northern fur seal is about 1.8 million animals, and approximately 70 percent of these seals are associated with Alaska's Pribilof Islands in the Bering Sea. The present population status of the northern fur seal herd is an international wildlife conservation/ management success story. Uncontrolled pelagic sealing (hunting on the open sea) had reduced the northern fur seal herd to an all-time low of about 250,000 animals shortly after the turn of the century. The U.S., in an effort to reverse the fur seal's population decline, negotiated a treaty between the U.S., USSR, Canada and Japan, which prohibited pelagic sealing and established quotas for the rookery harvests. Today northern fur seals are thriving once again and the international sealing agreement and research programs insure the continued viability and preservation of their population.

UTILIZATION: Northern fur seal pelts have been in demand for luxury garments since the 18th century. Harvesting operations are confined to controlled rookery hunts on Russia's Commander Islands and the U.S. owned Pribilof Islands. There is no public participation in the harvest, however it is often observed by tourists. The "stun and stick" method used to kill bachelor fur seals on the rookery has been extremely controversial even though veterinarians and medical technologists have concluded that the method being used is the most humane method practicable. Also, in 1977, a federal court ruled that the traditional method of killing fur seals was in fact humane. Almost the entire annual harvest (about 32,000 seal pelts) from all rookeries is processed in the U.S. and sold as preeminent luxury fur. Processed pelts have averaged $100 in value in recent years and some pelts were sold for as much as $300 each.

REFERENCES

ANONYMOUS. 1978. The Marine Mannal Protection Act of 1972. National Marine Fisheries Service. Annual Report, April 1, 1977 to March 31, 1978.

_____. 1977. The Story of the Pribilof Fur Seals. National Oceanic and Atmospheric Administration, U.S. Dept. of Commerce.

_____. 1965. Report on Investigations from 1958 to 1961. North Pacific Fur Seal Commission, Kenkyusha Co., Tokyo. 183 pp.

_____. 1969. Report on Investigations from 1964 to 1966. North Pacific Fur Seal Commission.

_____. 1971. Report on Investigations from 1962 to 1963. North Pacific Fur Seal Commission.

_____. 1975. Report on Investigations from 1967 to 1972. North Pacific Fur Seal Commission. Dependable Printing Co., Hyattsville, Maryland. 212 pp.

CHAPMAN, D. G. 1964. A Critical Study of Pribilof Fur Seal Population Estimates. U.S. Fish and Wildlife Service., Fish Bull. 63: 657-669.

JOHNSON, A. M. 1975. The Status of Northern Fur Seal Populations. In K. Ronald and A. W. Mansfield (Eds.) Biology of the Seal. Cons. Int. Expl. Mer., Proc. Verb., 169 p. RAPP P.-v Reun. CIEM. 169: 263-266.

KENYON, K. W., V. B. Sheffer and D. G. Chapman. 1954. A Population Study of the Alaska Fur Seal Herd. U.S. Fish and Wildlife Service, Spec. Sci. Rep. Wildl. 12, 77 pp.

KEYES, M. C. 1965. Pathology of the Northern Fur Seal. J. Am. Vet. Med. Assoc. 147: 1,090-1,095.

LANDER, R. H., and H. Kajimura. 1976. Status of Northern Fur Seals. Food Agricl. Organ. U.N., Adv. Comm. Mar. Resour. Res. FAO ACMRR/MM/SC/34, 50 pp.

ROPPEL, A. Y., A. M. Johnson, R. D. Bauer, D. G. Chapman, and F. Wilke. 1963. Fur Seal Investigations, Pribilof Islands, Alaska. U.S. Fish and Wildlife Service, Spec. Sci. Report. Fish. 454, 101 pp.

Map 28. **The Range of the Northern Fur Seal in Canada.**

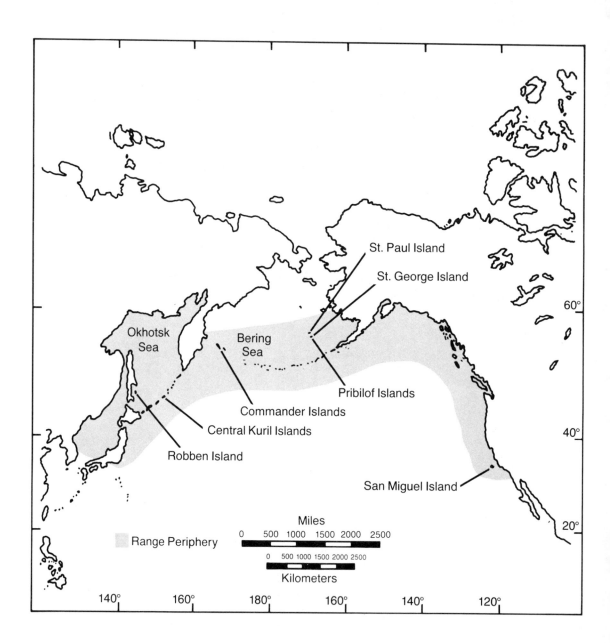

Female harp seal and pup.

HARP SEAL
(*Phoca groenlandica*)

DESCRIPTION: Harp seals owe their name to the irregular horseshoe-shaped band of black on the back of adult males. The black band crosses the shoulders, curves down toward the flanks and then turns up towards the hind flippers where it ends abruptly. The background color of the pelt is steel blue when wet and pale gray when dry. The head and tail are black, and the front flippers and belly are whitish. Adult females are similar in appearance to adult males except that the "harp" band and the head and tail are usually grayish-brown to black. Some adult females have irregular dark gray spots on their backs with no clearly defined "harp". Occasionally harp seals with dark sooty-colored coats occur. These melanistic color forms are usually males. Males are only slightly larger than females. Adult males reach lengths of 59 to 72 inches (150-184 cm) while adult females are 59 to 69 inches (150-174 cm) in length. Adult harp seals weigh from 187 to 419 pounds (85-190 kg). Adult weights fluctuate seasonally. The skull has 34 teeth. There are 2 mammae.

HABITAT: Harp seals inhabit the arctic and sub-arctic waters of the North Atlantic Ocean. They occur in 3 widely separated and distinct breeding populations — one in the White Sea, one in the "West Ice" near Jan Mayen Island (southwest of Spitsbergen), and one at Newfoundland. The Newfoundland population appears to be genetically isolated from the other stocks. It is divided into 2 interbreeding groups: one breeds on the southward drifting arctic pack ice off southern Labrador (called the "Front" population) and the other breeds on local ice in the Gulf of St. Lawrence (called the "Gulf" population).

FEEDING HABITS: Harp seals feed on a variety of fish and invertebrate prey, and their feeding habits vary with age and season. Young harp seals (beaters) in Newfoundland waters feed on small crustaceans, primarily euphausiids and shrimps. In the Arctic, during the summer, harp seals feed on capelin, polar cod and crustaceans, particularly amphipods and shrimps. Older harp seals feed chiefly on capelin and other pelagic fish such as herring and polar cod, and pelagic and benthic crustaceans including euphausiids, mysids, amphipods, and shrimps. Also, small quantities of benthic fish such as redfish, cod, American plaice and Greenland halibut are consumed.

BEHAVIOR: Harp seals are gregarious and highly migratory marine mammals. They "haul out" onto ice in dense herds to give birth, mate and molt. They also migrate and feed in loose herds. Harp seals dive to depths of 820 feet (250 m) and remain submerged for as long as 20 minutes while searching for food. Small prey such as capelin, shrimp and mysids are taken largely by sucking while larger fish are swallowed tail-first.

REPRODUCTION: Harp seals appear to be promiscuous and females are monestrous. Courtship and mating occur in late March, immediately after the females have finished nursing. Pregnant females haul onto the winter pack ice in late February or early March and, within a period of several days, give birth to a single pup. In each whelping area the seals usually are concentrated in 2 main groups. These groups occupy areas of 4 to 97 square miles (12-250 km²) and may contain as many as 2,000 adult females per ⅓ square mile (1 km²). Implantation is delayed for 2 to 3 months. After implantation the gestation period is approximately 9 months. At birth pups weigh about 24 pounds (11 kg). Pups are nursed for about 9 days before they are weaned and abandoned by their mothers. During this 9-day period, nursing pups more than triple their weight on milk which contains up to 45 percent fat. When weaned, pups weigh an average of 73 pounds (33 kg). One half of the weaned pups' weight is fat (blubber). At birth the pups are yellowish in color. In about 3 days the fur turns fluffy white and the pups are called "whitecoats". After about 18 days the natal coat is completely shed and replaced with a short-haired silvery one that is flecked with small dark spots. Pups with such coats are called "beaters". The succeeding juvenile coats are creamy brown with large dark blotches on the flanks, which often merge into a dark median band on the back. Juveniles with such coats are called "bedlamers" by sealers. Female harp seals reach sexual maturity between the ages of 4 and 6 years. Males do not attain sexual maturity until their seventh year or later.

POPULATION STATUS: During the post-war years, harp seal hunts caused a marked decline in the Newfoundland population of harp seals. This was primarily due to the large number of seals taken and the increased percentage of older seals in the harvest. Although historical data are inadequate for a precise assessment of the population's size prior to 1950, it is apparent that the reduction in herd size between 1950 and 1970 was about 50 to 60 percent (1 to 5 million seals) of the seals one year of age and older. Effective management practices were instituted in 1971 when the first catch quota was established. Since that time the population has steadily recovered and recent (1980) estimates indicate a pup production of 500,000 and a juvenile and adult population of about 2.0 million harp seals.

UTILIZATION: Harp seals have been hunted in Newfoundland since the early 1700s. The original method of capturing harp seals was netting (this method is still in limited use). The land-based netting operations were the primary method of sealing until the early 1800s when wooden sailing ships were used to hunt whitecoats and adult harp seals in offshore areas. In 1863 steam-powered wooden ships were employed for the offshore hunts and in 1906 steel-hulled vessels improved the sealers' ability to negotiate the ice flows and expanded the sealing operations. Today, as in the past, Canadian and Norwegian ships hunt primarily whitecoats while land-based sealers (landsmen) mainly hunt beaters, juveniles and adults. Fur, oil and meat are the principal products of the hunts. These products represent 76%, 10% and 14% respectively, of the income derived by Canadian sealers. Since 1978 the total allowable catch of harp seals has been 170,000 animals plus an allotment of 10,000 for the Canadian arctic and Greenland aboriginal hunts, for a total overall annual quota of 180,000 harp seals. Between 1978 and 1980 actual harvest ranged from 173,000 to 181,000 animals. Approximately 80% of the catch were whitecoats and 20% were juveniles and adults. Despite the controversy surrounding the harp seal hunts, the market value of the pelts has remained strong and relatively stable. The total value of harp seal furs and oil to Atlantic Canada was about 4.8 million dollars in 1980. Meat sales, primarily in Newfoundland, provided nearly $500,000 of additional income which increased the overall value of the 1980 harp seal harvest to over 5 million dollars.

REFERENCES

BANFIELD, A. W. F. 1974. The Mammals of Canada. Univ. Toronto Press, Toronto. 438 pp.

BOWEN, W.D., C.K. Capstick and D.E. Sergeant. 1981. Temporal Changes in the Reproductive Potential of Female Harp Seals (*Pagophilus groenlandicus*). Can. J. Fish. Aqua. Sci. 38: 495-503.

LAVIGNE, D.E. 1979. Management of Seals in the Northwest Atlantic Ocean. Trans. 44th North Amer. Wildl. Conf. p. 488-497.

ROFF, D., and W.D. Bowen. 1981. Population Dynamics of Harp Seals, 1967-1991. Northwest Atlantic Fisheries Organization SCR Doc. No. 81/XI/166/ 31 pp.

SERGEANT, D. E. 1976. History and Present Status of Populations of Harp and Hooded Seals. Biol. Conserv. 10: 95-118.

_____. 1965. Migrations of Harp Seals (*Pagophilus groenlandicus*) in the Northwest Atlantic. J. Fish Res. Bd. Canada. 22: 433-464.

WINTERS. G. H. 1978. Production, Mortality and Sustainable Yield of Northwest Atlantic Harp Seals (*Pagophilus groenlandicus*). J. Fish Res. Bd. Canada. 35: 1249-1261.

Map 29. **The Range of the Harp Seal in Canada.**

Jones Sd.
Lancaster Sd.
Thule
GREENLAND
ICELAND
Denmark Strait
Baffin Bay
Baffin Island
Davis Strait
Hudson Strait
Hudson Bay
NEWFOUNDLAND
Gulf of St. Lawrence

Miles
0   400   800

0   400   800
Kilometer

Range Periphery
Breeding Concentrations
Migration Routes

Male and female hooded seals. The male has extruded his septum like a balloon, as part of the courtship ritual.

HOODED SEAL
(*Cystophora cristata*)

DESCRIPTION: Adult male hooded seals are characterized by the large inflatable proboscis or "hood" which overhangs the upper lip. Females and immature males do not have hoods. The adult pelage is steel to bluish gray in background color with a pattern of large irregular black spots on the back and smaller spots on the neck and belly. The head and flippers are bluish-black, and the abdomen is whitish. The sexes are similar in appearance except males are considerably larger than females. Adult hooded seals range from 70 to 80 inches (177 - 250 cm) in length and weigh up to 882 pounds (400 kg). Like harp seals, hooded seal pups undergo pelage molts before attaining their adult coat. The skull has 30 teeth. There are 2 mammae.

HABITAT: The hooded seal, a pelagic species, inhabits the deep waters of the North Atlantic near the outer edge of the arctic ice pack. Three distinct breeding concentrations are known — one is located around Jan Mayen Island southeast of Spitsbergen, one in the Davis Strait and one at Newfoundland. The bulk of the Newfoundland breeding population occurs off the coast of southern Labrador, but a few breed in the Gulf of St. Lawrence. Hooded seals normally occur farther offshore than harp seals because hooded seals select very thick arctic ice for their haul-out sites.

FEEDING: Hooded seals feed on squid, octopus, redfish, cod, Greenland halibut, starfish, mussels and shrimps. The relative importance of these foods is unknown.

BEHAVIOR: Hooded seals are gregarious during the breeding, molting and migration periods, however hooded seals do not assemble in large congregations as do harp seals. During the breeding season, hooded seals aggregate in small groups which usually consist of an adult male, an adult female and her pup. Hooded seals are well-known for their aggressive behavior, especially when the pup is approached. When angered, males inflate their "hood," a pliable internasal septum, which is a red balloon-shaped structure. After whelping adult hooded seals travel north, migrating from West Greenland around Cape Farewell in early May and up the east coast of Greenland to the Denmark Strait where in mid-summer they molt on arctic ice. Here they are joined by the westward migrating herds from the Jan Mayen area. The migration routes of the Davis Strait herd are not yet known. After molting the seals disperse on feeding forays.

REPRODUCTION: Hooded seals appear to be promiscuous with as any as 7 males competing for a receptive female. Females are monestrous and, like harp seals, the hooded seal exhibits a post-partum mating and delayed implantation for about 3 months. Parturition occurs in late March and only one pup is produced per litter. Pups weigh about 50 pounds (23 kg) at birth and they have shed their foetal white coat before birth. Newborn (bluebacks) have a slate-blue back, a blackish head and silvery-white underparts which are sharply demarcated from the blue back along the flanks. The lactation (nursing) period in hooded seals is shorter than in harp seals, and may only last 7 days. Females become sexually mature at 3 to 4 years of age, but males do not become sexually mature until after they are 4 years old.

POPULATION STATUS: The Jan Mayen breeding herd is the largest concentration of hooded seals in the entire population. Apparently, excessive hunting has caused a continuous decline in that herd in recent years. In 1956 pup production was estimated to be 95,000 animals but in 1979, production was down to an estimated 50,000 pups. In 1977, the catch quota was reduced in an attempt to increase pup production to a more desirable level. Recent estimates of the Newfoundland breeding herd indicate a relatively constant level of production at about 27,000 pups annually during the 1970s. The juvenile and adult proportion of that herd appears to be about 100,000 animals. The Davis Strait herd is not commercially hunted and population levels and trends are unknown, but several preliminary aerial surveys indicate that it is probably smaller than the Newfoundland herd.

UTILIZATION: The breeding herd of hooded seals off the coast of Newfoundland has been hunted since the early 1800s when the offshore harvest of harp seals was initiated. Since 1975, a quota of 15,000 animals has been used to regulate the harvest of that herd and the kill of females is limited to 5 percent of the daily catch to regulate the number of females in the total harvest. The Jan Mayen herd has been over-harvested since 1946. The catch quota of 30,000 seals has been reduced recently (by about 30%) as a conservation measure. Land-based Greenland fisherman hunt migrating hooded seals for fur, oil and meat and during the summer months. The primary products of the hooded seal hunts are fur and oil. Other than carcasses used by Newfoundland sealers and a more general use of pup flippers, hooded seal meat is not generally used by sealers. The "blueback's" coat is the most highly valued hooded seal pelt and, like the harp seal's whitecoat pelt, it is used in the manufcture of fur coats. Between 1978 and 1980 an average of 12,600 hooded seals were harvested annually from the Newfoundland herd. About 50 percent of these were taken by Canadian sealers, for a total value of about $350,000 annually.

REFERENCES

BANFIELD, A. W. F. 1974. The Mammals of Canada. Univ. Toronto Press, Toronto. 438 pp.

ORITSLAND, T. 1964. The Breeding Biology of the Female Hooded Seal. Fiskets Gang. 50: 5-19.

RASMUSSEN, B. 1960. On the Stock of Hood Seals in the Northern Atlantic. [Transl. from Norwegian] Fisken og Havet. No. 1. 23 pp.

SERGEANT, D. E. 1976. History and Present Status of Populations of Harp and Hooded Seals. Biol. Conserv. 10:95-118.

———. 1974. A Rediscovered Whelping Population of Hooded Seals (*Cystophora cristata*) Erxleben and its Possible Relationship to Other Populations. Polarforshung. 44:1-7

WINTERS. G. H., and B. Bergflodt. 1978. Mortality and Productivity of the Newfoundland Hooded Seal Stock. ICNAF Res. Doc. 78/XI/91 (Revised).

Map 30.

**The Range of the Hooded Seal
in Canada.**

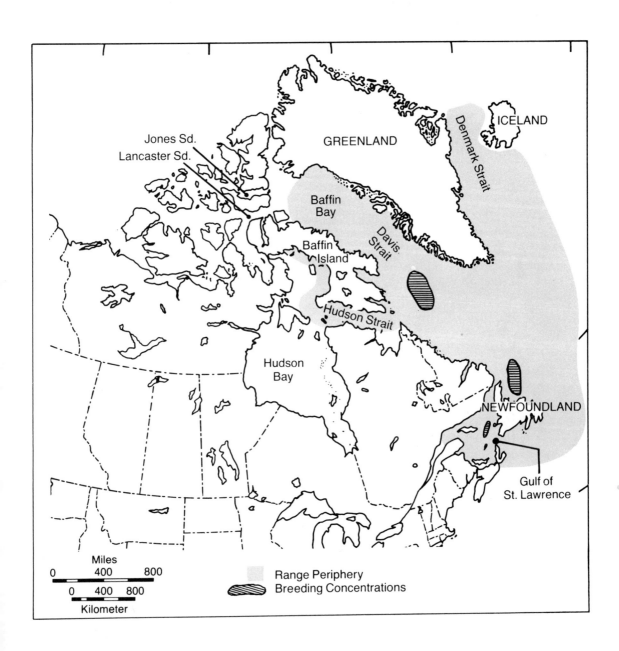

Miles
0   400   800

0   400   800
Kilometer

Range Periphery
Breeding Concentrations

ICELAND

GREENLAND

Denmark Strait

Jones Sd.
Lancaster Sd.

Baffin
Bay

Davis
Strait

Baffin
Island

Hudson Strait

Hudson
Bay

NEWFOUNDLAND

Gulf of
St. Lawrence

NOTES

The following pages are for your use in keeping notes.

NOTES

NOTES

NOTES

NOTES

NOTES